D1383042

100 WAYS TO WIN A TEN-SPOT

100 ways to win a
TEN-SPOT

scams, cons, games you can't lose

PAUL ZENON

CHICAGO
REVIEW
PRESS

Text © Carlton Books Limited 2003
Design and illustrations © Carlton Books Limited 2003
Design and project art direction: Darren Jordan
Illustrations: Peter Liddiard, Sudden Impact Media; Darren Jordan
Cover design: Joan Sommers Design
All rights reserved
This edition has been fully Americanized and differs from the British edition in
some respects.
Published in 2007 by
Chicago Review Press, Incorporated
814 North Franklin Street
Chicago, Illinois 60610
ISBN-13: 978-1-55652-642-8
ISBN-10: 1-55652-642-3
Printed in the United States of America
5 4 3 2 1

DEDICATION

This book is dedicated to Bill Thompson of the House of Secrets, friend and mentor for the past thirty years and the nicest guy you're ever likely to meet. Thanks, Bill.

CONTENTS

TRICKS AND BETS FOR USE IN BARS AND CLUBS, DESIGNED TO SEPARATE THOSE
WITH A BELLY FULL OF BOOZE AND BRAVADO FROM THEIR SWEET GREEN.

TWO TIPPED OFF *37–65*

THERE IS SUCH A THING AS A FREE LUNCH. YOU'LL NEVER HAVE TO PAY FOR ANOTHER MEAL AGAIN USING THESE CULINARY CONS. THEY SEEM FAIR, BUT YOUR OPPONENT ALWAYS LOSES AND HAS TO PICK UP THE BILL.

THREE SPORTING CHANCE

CAN'T SHUFFLE A PACK WITHOUT PLAYING 52-CARD PICK UP? NEVER PICKED UP A POOL CUE IN YOUR LIFE? FUMBLE NO MORE. HERE ARE THE REAL SECRETS OF THE SHARPS, SHARKS, AND HUSTLERS; WITHOUT ANY SKILL WHATSOEVER YOU'LL BE ABLE TO BEAT THE EXPERTS AT THEIR OWN GAME.

FOUR MASTERMIND

DO YOU HIDE EVERY TIME A BAR QUIZ STARTS OR SOMEONE SUGGESTS A GAME OF TRIVIAL PURSUIT? NOT ANY MORE. CONCEAL YOUR IGNORANCE WITH THESE TRICKY QUESTIONS GUARANTEED TO PUZZLE YOUR OPPONENT, KNOCK THE QUIZMASTER OFF HIS PERCH, AND EARN YOURSELF ENOUGH MONEY TO PAY FOR A PROPER EDUCATION.

FIVE PARTY ANIMAL

CAN'T SING, CAN'T DANCE? DON'T WORRY, THESE SCAMS AND SWINDLES ARE DESIGNED TO MAKE YOU THE LIFE AND SOUL OF THE PARTY, WINNING THE ADMIRATION OF THE MASSES, NOT TO MENTION THEIR HARD-EARNED CASH.

"SON, NO MATTER HOW FAR YOU TRAVEL AND HOW MUCH YOU SEE,
SOMEDAY, SOMEWHERE, SOME GUY IS GOING TO COME UP TO YOU WITH
A BRAND NEW DECK OF CARDS ON WHICH THE SEAL HAS NEVER EVEN
BEEN BROKEN, AND HE IS GOING TO OFFER TO BET YOU THAT THE QUEEN OF
HEARTS WILL JUMP OUT OF THAT DECK AND SQUIRT CIDER IN YOUR EAR.
BUT SON, DO NOT BET WITH THIS MAN FOR, AS SURE AS YOU DO,
YOU ARE GOING TO END UP WITH AN EAR FULL OF CIDER."

— DAMON RUNYAN

INTRODUCTION

Paul Zenon's *100 Ways to Win a Ten-Spot* is a comprehensive guide to scams and swindles that will make you a winner every time. Unlike magic tricks, these bets and stunts use everyday objects and require no skill – just balls. Within minutes you too can be the life, and scourge, of the party, scamming the pants off everyone in sight!

They say that cheaters never prosper. Unfortunately (or, rather, fortunately, now that you're in possession of this book), that just ain't true. Most likely it was a rumor spread to ease the mind of some poor sucker who had just lost for the umpteenth time in a rigged game of cards. The real truth is that, armed with the right knowledge, a cheater will always win. He doesn't take chances. What he does take is your money, quicker than you can say I.O.U.

Paul Zenon is the U.K.'s favorite fun-loving criminal. Over the years he has worked as a magician, comedian, croupier, and small-time conman. He has spent a lifetime hanging out with and studying the techniques of a rogue's gallery of tricksters, shysters, frauds, sharks, and snake-oil sellers. In this, his insider's guide, he spills the beans, reveals the tricks of his trade, and gives us a crash course in cheating – cheating at cards, at pool, and in pub quizzes, drinking games, and bar bets, in fact anywhere and everywhere that you can corner a sucker into chancing his hard-earned dough on what seems like a perfectly fair bet. Of course there's no such thing as a fair bet – at least not in this book. Every game and wager is rigged in your favor. And why not? Casinos and bookies have been doing it for years. Remember, knowledge is power, and this knowledge is hard-won. Use it wisely! ♠

100 WAYS TO WIN A TEN-SPOT

ONE

THE DRINKS ARE ON YOU

"NEVER GIVE A SUCKER
AN EVEN BREAK."
— PHINEAS T. BARNUM

1 BOTTOMS UP

THE HOOK

Few people know it, but you are the world's fastest drinker. No, really. Your friends aren't convinced, but you keep on bragging until they're sick of hearing about it.

"Okay then, a five-spot says I'm way faster than you. In fact, a five-spot says I can drink three pints before you can even drink three shots!"

Few people can resist a bet, especially when they've had a few. So it won't be long before someone takes you up on your challenge.

"And just to make it interesting," you say, "the loser pays for all the drinks as well — fair enough?"

So, how exactly are you going to drink three pints before your friend drinks the same number of shots? Very easily is the answer.

THE CATCH

Get the drinks lined up in two rows and then crank up the pressure.

"Are you sure you can afford it?" No one likes to feel cheap and no one likes to back down after accepting a challenge.

"Well, let's make it a ten-spot then." You've cornered him now, but there will be a trickle of suspicion running through his mind, so you reassure him, while at the same time setting up the very rules that will make you a winner.

"And just to make sure everything's fair, we're not allowed to touch each other's glasses, or each other; no nudging elbows or anything like that. And no one else is allowed to touch either of us or our glasses. To give me a sporting chance, the only thing I'd ask is that you let me finish my first pint before you start on the shots. Is that okay?"

Of course it's okay. You couldn't possibly manage another two pints in the time he can down three shots, especially when you've just slammed one.

Next step: *get the money.* This is an essential part of any scam. Hand over your cash to a neutral party and get your opponent to do the same. It's another rule of the bar bet. No one likes to pay, so you've got to see the color of the money first.

Now you're ready. Get Mr. Neutral to shout "Go!" and, as soon as you hear it, pick up your first pint and down it as fast as you can. Down in one – don't drown yourself. As soon as you're finished, put your glass upside down right over one of his full shot glasses. Now you can take your time drinking the remaining two pints. You've already won.

Why? Because you made the rule that no one could touch any of the glasses. Since your glass is covering one of his – which you didn't touch – he can never down that final shot.

Enjoy the rest of the night.

❷ BUCKS IN

THE HOOK

There's no football on TV, the karaoke machine is busted, and it's Sara the bartender's day off. The bar couldn't get any duller. At least that's what you thought until Sid "The Kid" walks in and starts telling everyone about how many unsafe cars he's sold that day. If he'd turned the clocks back any further, that Cavalier would have had to have been driven by cavaliers. But all is not lost; he's got a few bucks on him, and you, due to a horse with three legs being unexpectedly entered into the 3:30 at Arlington Park, are broke. Time to replenish your funds.

You take your last ten-spot out of your pocket, roll it up, throw it high in the air, and catch it in your empty pint glass. And you keep doing it until you've caught Sid's attention. And when he asks what the hell you're doing, you say, "Just practicing."

"Practicing for what, being institutionalized?"

"Practicing catching this ten-spot in this glass. A guy at the Fool and Bladder said it couldn't be done."

"Said what couldn't be done?" asks Sid.

"Said I couldn't throw the ten-spot three feet in the air and catch it in this glass. Said he'd give me a ten-spot for every one I could do."

"Looks easy to me," says Sid, understandably puzzled.

"Nah, takes coordination. I bet you couldn't do it."

Sid looks at you as if you are stupid. And as soon as you get that look you follow through, saying, "In fact, I'll give you a buck for every bill you catch."

It sounds foolhardy but it's a bet you can't lose.

THE CATCH

Get Sid to open his wallet, take out some ten-spots, and scrunch them up into balls. Arrange them along the bar. Now borrow some pint glasses from the bartenders and put one next to each rolled up bill. Meanwhile, you will also need to get some dollar bills. Yes, you will be paying out, but no, you won't be losing.

The bet is exactly as you said it would be. Sid has to throw each note at least three feet in the air and then catch it in a pint glass.

At the end of the session, he'll probably have all the notes in all the glasses. Take each glass in turn and pour out the notes. Count them aloud and then announce the score.

"That's six you got in the glasses. Fantastic. And like I said, I'll give you a buck for every one you caught. Here's your six bucks, pal."

Push six dollar bills toward him and then add, "And I guess these are mine. Like I said, a buck for every one."

The laughter of everyone's ridicule should drown out his protests. This place seems to be getting a bit livelier at last. But time to move on. There are a dozen bars to visit and a sucker like Sid in every one of them.

❸ UNDER COVER OPERATION

THE HOOK

You don't have to play every bet for big money. Sometimes it's easier to take it off 'em in nickels and dimes rather than rolls of bills. This one will keep you in free drinks all night if only because your friends will watch it over and over again as new people join your group.

While you are waiting for the rest of your motley crew to arrive at the bar, make the following wager with whoever seems to be the most gullible. Jim's always a good bet. His parents didn't give him an easy-to-spell name for nothing. "Did you know, Jim, that these tables are actually porous?" Knock on the table like you're testing the wood.

"Porous?" says Jim, genuinely interested because it's a rare day when anyone addresses him by name.

"Porous. Liquid goes right through it like a sponge. I'll show you what I mean."

You take Jim's whiskey and Coke – he's a slow drinker and one drink usually lasts him all night – and you place it in the center of the table. Then you say, "Wait there a minute," go to the bar, and borrow a cocktail shaker, ice bucket, vase – anything that isn't see-through and will fit over the glass.

Jim will wonder what you are doing placing an ice bucket over his drink, but he won't have to wonder for too long. Here's the pitch: "I bet you a buck that I can drink that whiskey and Coke without lifting the bucket – won't touch the bucket, won't move the bucket, won't do anything at all to it. But I'll drink your drink."

Even Jim, the most cautious guy this side of a minefield, will have to concede that this is impossible and might just be worth a buck to see. With a nudge and a hint that "it's only for fun," you'll soon have him begging you to prove your claim. And, amazingly, you can.

THE CATCH

When Jim produces his money and places it alongside yours on the table, you reiterate your boast: "I won't touch the bucket. Won't lift the bucket. Won't move the bucket. That clear?" Crystal. You then dive under the table and proceed to make the most disgusting slurping noises you can. Jim will start to think about the "porous" wood remark you made earlier. Surely you can't be drinking it through the wood. Can you?

Come back up smacking your lips and saying, "Next time don't drown it with so much Coke." Sit down, like the smug person that you are, pick up the money from the table and gaze off into the distance. It might take a minute or two, but curiosity is an impatient bedfellow and Jim will have no option but to lift the bucket to see if his drink is still there.

It is. But Jim has unwittingly done you the favor of removing the bucket. Quickly, pick up the glass and down its contents in one. You've made good on your promise and drunk the whiskey without touching the bucket. Let's hope he didn't really drown it with Coke.

That's a buck and a drink for you. What's more, Jim will be more than happy for you to play the same trick for the rest of the night on every person that comes anywhere near; it'll help him to feel less of a sucker himself. Until next time, that is.

4 DOWN AND OUT

THE HOOK

Poor Jim. He was the first to be taken and now he's going to be the last. There should be a law against it really, but fortunately there isn't.

He's been watching you closely, betting everyone that you can drink their drinks without touching that there bucket. If only he had the balls to do that, he's thinking. In fact, that's what everyone who's lost money to you will be thinking. Perhaps they'll try it themselves one day.

Well, no time like the present. The bar's about to close and last call has been announced. You lean over to Jim and say, "You've got to give it a try Jim. You'll regret it if you don't."

"You reckon?"

"You've watched me do it all night, haven't you?"

"Yes but...."

"No buts, Jim. This night is yours."

And with that you pull over a total stranger who is carrying his drink from the bar. "Hey, excuse me, but you've just got to see this. My buddy here's got a fantastic trick, right, Jim?"

THE CATCH

As I said, poor Jim. Nervously he repeats your proposition to a man he's never met before. And he claims that he can drink the man's drink even though it is hidden under that bucket. He won't lift the bucket, won't move the bucket, won't touch the bucket. And here's the buck to say he can do it.

Be gentle. It's Jim's first time. Help him set the bucket over the stranger's drink and give him a nod of reassurance just before he ducks under the table and starts to make his slurping noises.

But as soon as he does, you raise your finger to your lips and shush the crowd as you quietly lift the bucket. Now, you quickly down the drink and replace the bucket.

Jim resurfaces to a smiling crowd. He thinks he's pulled off the trick successfully. Until the stranger, your instant stooge, lifts the bucket. No one is more stunned than Jim to find the glass empty. I've seen victims speechless when they discover that the drink has indeed disappeared from beneath that bucket. Which is just as well, considering the world of pain they are about to enter as they try to explain the trick away.

⑤ SIX SHOOTER

THE HOOK

What I like about bar bets is that they are all about lateral thinking. And, fortunately for us, after a couple of beers most people can't even spell the phrase, never mind put it into action.

Most bar bets are simple puzzles. Stuff a kid could solve. But the best ones are not so much brain teasers as devices to encourage an individual's public humiliation while simultaneously emptying his or her wallet. Take this one for instance.

You take six shot glasses, three of them full and three of them empty. And you arrange them in a line so that the three full glasses are on the left of the row and the three empty glasses on the right. So far so easy. But here's the wager.

"I bet you a ten you can't move the glasses around so that they alternate, full/empty/full/empty all the way along the row." To demonstrate what you mean, you openly rearrange the glasses so that they do indeed alternate full/empty. Seems easy. You did it, why can't they?

The reason is simple. You just shuffled the glasses around but to win the bet they are only allowed to move one of them. Alternate the glasses by only moving one glass. Looks impossible but it's not. Still, it'll cost them ten bucks to find out how to do it. Loser pays for the drinks, too. No prizes for guessing who that's going to be.

THE CATCH

I regret to say that this is simplicity itself. It's that lateral thinking I mentioned earlier. To win, all you need do is lift up the center one of the full glasses and pour its contents into the center glass of the empty ones. Hey presto, the glasses now alternate.

⑥ THREES UP

THE HOOK

The six glasses in *Six Shooter* might prove too much for some folks. Six is a big number if you've had four pints of Old Scrotum's Special or whatever the real ale nerds have christened beer of the week. So try this, with just three shot glasses.

Take the three glasses and arrange them in a line on the table. When someone asks what you are doing, say, "It's a sobriety test. Cop once showed it to me." Quickly you take two of the glasses, one in each hand, and flip them over top to bottom. Then you do it again, switching glasses. And then a third time. All the glasses finish mouth upwards. "See? Sober as a judge."

The lawman in question must have been Judge Pickled because as your pals know, you've had more than your fair share for the evening. Still, you set the glasses up again and start turning them two at a time until they're once again all mouth uppermost. "Ready to be filled," you point out.

"Want another?"

They certainly do, and that's when you decide to make things a little more interesting. "Tell you what. If you pass the sobriety test, I'll get the drinks. Better still, I'll give you ten bucks and you can go and get them yourself. But if you don't pass it, the drinks are on you."

The so-called test seems to consist of nothing more than turning glasses over two at a time, three times in total, so that they all end up mouth uppermost.

They've seen you do it twice – it looks totally easy – and they will already be feeling confident. But to make sure, you do it a third time, saying, "It's really very simple. You just have to turn two glasses at a time and you're only allowed three turns. All glasses ready to be filled at the finish. Got that? Okay, who wants to give it a go?"

Well who could possibly refuse a simple challenge like that? No one who's already filled up on Old Scrotum's Special, that's for sure.

THE CATCH

This is a real classic of the genre and many a sober man has found his wallet lightened because of it. That's because you cheat.

You begin by demonstrating how simple the test is with the three glasses in a row as shown. The middle one is mouth upwards and the outer ones are mouth downwards.

♠ Make your first move by taking glasses B and C, one in each hand, and turning them over at the same time.

♠ Make your second move by turning over glasses A and C.

♠ Make your third and final move by turning over glasses B and C. That brings all three glasses mouth up.

You can repeat these moves several times but do it quickly as if you are trying to confuse them. Once they think they have it, you put the glasses back in their starting position. At least you appear to.

In fact you put them in the totally opposite position to the one you started with. The middle one mouth downwards and the end two mouth up.

If your victim starts with the glasses in this arrangement, there is no way he can bring the glasses mouth up in three moves. Which, as always, means he'll be the one filling the glasses. Enjoy.

❶ HIGH SPIRITS

THE HOOK

Some things are worth paying to see. Really! This is one bet that everyone will be trying the day after you show it to them. It just seems so amazing that it works at all. Makes you wish you'd paid more attention in science class.

"Here's something you'll never forget," you say, taking a shot glass full of whiskey and a shot glass full of water and placing them on the bar. "Do you think that I can get the whiskey and the water to change places, just like that?"

Let your victim consider it for a moment. He'll have a dozen questions and you can answer them all honestly.

"No, what I'm saying is that I can make the whiskey and the water change places. And I'm not going to do it by pouring the whiskey into another glass. In fact, I won't use any other glasses. Just these two here."

Pause while the victim considers the options and then eventually tells you that frankly he can't see you making good on that claim. That's the time to hit him with a friendly wager. Friendly as in "friendly fire."

"Well, ten bucks says I can. Ten bucks says I can get the whiskey from this glass into that. And the water from that glass into this." Put your tenner on the table, a direct challenge to his manhood.

Now the first thing anyone wants to do is avoid risking any money. But this is a money game. No money, no miracle. So don't be tempted to give a free show. You're not a registered charity. Instead, turn the whole thing around. Tell him that he was the one who didn't believe you could do it, and if that's the way he feels he should put his money where his mouth is. In other words, wind him up until you hear the spring strain, because when he finally puts his cash on the table, it's as good as yours.

THE CATCH

As I said before, he'll probably thank you for this one. All you need to do it beside the glasses of whiskey and water is a slim, laminated membership card of some sort. Doesn't matter what it is as long as it is waterproof and big enough to cover the mouth of one of the glasses.

Here's what you do. First of all, make sure that the whiskey glass is full to the brim. The glass of water should be filled just shy of the top.

Now place the laminated card over the mouth of the whiskey glass. Very carefully lift the glass and card together and turn them upside down. The card keeps the whiskey in the glass. Place the whiskey glass and card over the glass of water.

Make sure the glasses are aligned perfectly. Now slowly and gradually move the card to one side so that a tiny opening appears between the glasses on the inside. The miracle that follows is guaranteed to amaze even cynical old you. You see, the whiskey is heavier than the water, and it will begin to seep into the lower glass. In response, the water will be forced into the upper glass. Incredible as it may seem, the whiskey and water are changing place before your very eyes. David Copperfield would be proud of you.

When all the whiskey is in the bottom glass, pick up your winnings and buy yourself a well-earned drink.

8 UP AND AWAY

THE HOOK

"It can't be done," you say to your friends around the bar. "It just can't." You have, of course, carefully engineered this conversation for the benefit of Mike who happened to be passing by at that very moment. You wouldn't have bothered were it not for the fact that you heard Mike had some luck with a filly at Del Mar and has so much sweet green in his pocket that he rustles as he walks.

"It just can't be done," you say again. Mike has stopped and is looking at you as if you can't be trusted, which, of course, you can't. He's wary of your games, but a man who has just won on the horses tends to think himself invincible when it comes to the laws of probability. And anyway, he'll only pour his winnings into that slot machine, so really you're about to do him and the economy a big favor by keeping his money in circulation for a little longer. At least, that's how we like to think of it.

"Mike, it's simple. I say that you can't lift a shot of whiskey from the table without spilling a drop." It's a stupid claim. Anyone can do that, thinks Mike. "What's the catch?"

"No catch. I bet you ten bucks that I can place a glass of whiskey on the bar, right here, and you can't lift it without spilling a drop. No catch, but there are conditions."

Mike wonders what they are, expecting something tricky as usual.

"No tricks. Conditions are you only use one hand and you lift the drink straight up. Just reach out and lift the drink up, like this."

You demonstrate with the empty glass. Mike thinks about it. And you turn that thought into a wager by saying, "I'll even buy the whiskey, and you can have it after the bet, win or lose. Can't be fairer than that. All you've got to do is lift up the glass of whiskey without spilling any. How does that sound?"

With a pocketful of money it doesn't sound too bad, especially as you are buying the whiskey. At least he can console himself with that if he loses. Can't he?

THE CATCH

Poor Mike. He doesn't even get to drink the whiskey in this one.

Have the glass filled with a single shot of whiskey and place it on the bar. Repeat the conditions of the bet, reminding Mike and everyone else that he must only use one hand and lift the glass straight up. Get him to say that he understands and accepts the wager. And make sure he hands over his tenner to a third party for safekeeping because after he has seen what is going to happen, he might not appreciate the way you won.

With everything set, you quickly take out the laminated card you used in *High Spirits*, place it on top of the glass, invert it, and set the glass on the bar top. Now carefully slide the laminated card from underneath it. There is now an upside-down glass of whiskey on the bar. And there's no way that Mike can lift it without spilling its contents everywhere. Told you Mike wouldn't be getting that drink. You, however, are perfectly entitled to his ten bucks.

A good tip is to have a bar towel handy when you perform this stunt — there's going to be a certain amount of mopping up to do when that glass eventually gets lifted, and you don't want to be making life difficult for the bartender; in the world of the bar scammer, he's an essential ally.

⑨ FOLLOW THE LEADER

THE HOOK

The evening is in full swing, it's your round next, and your wallet is distinctly on the anorexic side. You pick on a likely victim and suggest that the two of you play a drinking game — everyone loves a drinking game and it can be a great decoy for an out-and-out scam. Loser pays for the next round, obviously.

"It's very simple," you explain. "All you've got to do is follow what I do. Ready?" Although no contracts have been signed, your about-to-be-suckered friend is already nodding his head. After all, it would be churlish not to play along.

"Okay, pick up your glass." He does, but you make sure he picks it up in exactly the same way you do. "Pay attention. You've got to follow me exactly. Pick the glass up in your right hand. Remember, loser buys the drinks."

Now that the rules are set, you take him through a simple and slightly bizarre ritual. You raise your glass of beer to the heavens and shout, "To Odin!" He follows suit.

Then you raise the glass to the right and shout, "To the sun!" He does the same.

You raise your glass to the left and shout, "To the moon!" And again, like sheep, he follows.

Then you bring the glass to your lips and take a big swig. So does your drinking buddy.

You raise your glass once again, shouting, "To the Mighty Thor!" and for no good reason so does your pal. Then raise the glass to the right saying, "To the rain!" and then to the left, "To the wind!"

Then you take another sip. And raise the glass once more directly in front of you — but this time say nothing.

And no matter how closely your friend has been following you, he will not be able to follow the next move. The lemming has been driven to the edge of the cliff and is about to be given a nudge.

THE CATCH

This is beautifully simple. When you take that last mouthful of beer, keep it in your mouth – do not swallow it. That's why when you raise the glass a third time you don't say anything. You can't – your mouth is full. And that's what makes the last move possible.

Raise the drink again to the right and then to the left. Then slowly bring it back, hold it in front of your mouth, and spit the beer back out in a stream into the glass. Your victim won't be able to duplicate this, having automatically swallowed his. That next round is on him.

TWICE SHY

THE HOOK

The saying that a little knowledge is a dangerous thing is never more true than when it comes to bar bets. There you are, having a great time in the local pub, when trouble arrives in the shape of Smart-Ass Stan. It was all going so well – you've managed to pull three or four of your favourite stunts and never had to open your wallet once. You're drinking for free and enjoying every minute of it. But here comes Stan. The same Stan that watched you go through your entire repertoire of scams and swindles just a week ago. Stan, who lost not once, not twice, but three times to your shenanigans and only paid up when your pal Mad Mike threatened to use him as a bar towel. Yes, Stan is here, clued up and looking for revenge. But there's no man so blind as knows a little. And with that in mind you invite the whole group to play *Follow the Leader*.

Stan, with a glint in his eye, will assume you have forgotten that he was one of the losers in the *Follow the Leader* game not a week ago. He knows its secret, and, sure of winning and gaining revenge, he happily plays along.

Glasses are raised and toasts made. First to Odin, then the sun and the moon. Then to the Mighty Thor and the wind and the rain. And then you drink and spit and everyone laughs. All except for Stan, because Stan spits too. He grins triumphantly – he's won! Oh no he hasn't.

THE CATCH

The reason Stan won't win is that you then unexpectedly raise the glass again. You raise it high in the air then make another silent toast to the right and then to the left. You bring the glass to your lips once again and then, to Stan's amazement and intense irritation, spurt out a second stream of beer.

The explanation is simple. First time around you only spit out half of your mouthful. But Stan spat out all of his. He's cashed his chips in early, so to speak, leaving you the victor. The moral of the story is never try to con a conman.

⑪ BOTTLE BANK

THE HOOK

One sure way of getting money out of a sucker is to offer to show him how to do a trick with it. Now he has no excuse. If he wants to see the trick, he has to put up the cash. The cash in this case is our old pal, the ubiquitous ten-dollar bill, which you take from him as you explain the rules of the game.

"It's a game of skill," you say, lying. "Some people can do it, some people can't. I can do it, but I'll bet you can't."

You are being deliberately arrogant. No one likes a smart-ass, especially when they're in possession of their tenner. "In fact, I'm so sure that you can't do it, I'm prepared to bet you a ten-spot. I'll put up my ten against yours."

At this stage the sucker might like to see the color of your money. Take out a bill and hand it to a completely independent third party; preferably your best friend. No point taking any chances.

Put the sucker's ten-spot flat on the table and then borrow an empty beer bottle, turn it upside-down, and stand it mouth downwards on the ten-dollar bill. The bottle should be on the center of the bill, pinning it down on the table.

"Here's the bet. All you have to do is whip the ten-dollar bill free without knocking over the bottle. You can touch the bill but you're not allowed to touch the bottle. Now I'm warning you it's difficult so be careful. Bob — better move to one side because from where I'm standing it looks like you're in the direct line of fire.

"To make it fair, I'll give you three chances, okay? The only thing is, remember you can't touch the bottle."

Whether it is okay or not, the sucker's bill is stuck under the bottle and if he wants it back, he's got to take you up on your bet.

Giving him three chances to snatch the bill from under the bottle without knocking it over may seem a bit generous. It's not. If he's depending on pure skill or a knack to get his money back, he's going to fail. Brains are what are needed here but if you've chosen your victim correctly, you'll have picked someone that doesn't have an excess of gray matter.

THE CATCH

It's all a matter of suggestion. When you made the bet you talked about whipping away the bill. You asked Bob to stand back in order to avoid any accident involving flying glassware. And, you might even have jerked your hand back to suggest a possible reckless attempt to yank the bill free. Subliminal suggestion, all of it. The sucker will never be able to pull the bill free.

Slow stealth is what is required. After the sucker has toppled the bottle three times, you prove it can be done as follows.

You very carefully start to roll up the bill at one of the short ends. Take it slow and easy and continue rolling the bill until it meets the bottle. Move slower still as you continue rolling. You'll be surprised to see that the bottle is pushed by the rolled up portion of the tenner, little by little, along the length of the bill until it finally slides off the far end, coming to rest on the tabletop. The bill is free. It's also yours. Cheers.

12 MOUTH TO MOUTH

THE HOOK

They say money talks, but all it's saying to your victims is "Bye." Here's another slim chance for them to win back what was already theirs to start with.

This time you'll need two empty beer bottles in addition to another borrowed ten-dollar bill. You stand one of the bottles on the table and then place the bill on top of it. Makes sure it's a nice crisp bill, not one that's wrinkled beyond recognition. On top of the bill, you place the second bottle, mouth to mouth with the first. The bill is trapped between them.

The bet is the same as before. If the sucker can get the bill free, he can claim one of yours along with it. If he doesn't, you take his. Once again, he's not allowed to touch the bottles, only the bill.

If the punter has already seen you work *Bottle Bank* he might be tempted to try the rolling-up maneuver. If so, good luck to him. I've never got it to work. He might even try to yank the bill free, in the traditional tablecloth-from-under-the-plates style. If the bill was held by the bottles near one of its ends, that might work. But it isn't. The bill is trapped at its very center. If anyone does intend to depend on their catlike reflexes to whip the bill away, you'd be advised to post outfielders around the table to catch the flying debris.

THE CATCH

Brains score over brawn once again in this money-grabbing caper. It's perfectly true that any attempt to tug the bill from between the two bottles will pretty much be guaranteed to result in failure. But remember what I said about it working if the bill was gripped just by its edge? Well, that's the secret of the stunt.

When it comes to your turn you gently and openly tear right across the bill. Now the bottles do grip it near its newly ripped edge.

Grip the trapped bill at the other end with the thumb and forefinger of one hand. You need a really firm grip.

Extend the forefinger of the other hand and bring it down sharply with a chopping motion on the new middle of the bill. If you do it fast and clean the bill will be snapped away and the bottles will remain standing.

Your reward for this feat of dexterity is in two pieces but a strip of Scotch tape will soon put that right. The ten-dollar bill will certainly be easier to mend than your victim's ego.

One last word of warning. This swindle takes practice. So do make sure you try it at home before you attempt it in public. Unless I'm in the bar, of course. I like a good laugh.

⑬ CRASH THE ASH

THE HOOK

This one was shown to me by my great Uncle Harold who, when a round of drinks was called for, was always the first to put his hand into his pocket . . . and leave it there.

I can't ever remember him buying a round and yet he was the drunkest man I ever knew. What better testimonial to his scam expertise could you wish for? But I do remember him showing me this cunning little stunt. It was the best ten-spot I ever spent.

Begin by placing a brandy glass on the table and a coaster on top of it. Then borrow a cigarette (you forgetfully left yours at home) and balance it vertically, filter end at the bottom, in the center of the coaster. Finally, place a small coin on top of it.

Conclude the arrangements by finding yourself a sucker with more money than sense and making the following wager.

"Here's the problem. And it's worth a ten-spot if you can solve it. All you have to do is get the coin into the brandy glass. That's the easy bit. The difficult bit is getting it in there without touching the coin or the cigarette or the glass."

"Can you touch the coaster?" someone will ask. "Absolutely not," you reply, happy that someone has taken the bait. "Just can't touch the coin, cigarette, glass, or coaster. Any takers?"

You make the offer as if it's a party trick but as soon as someone steps forward to take up the challenge you deftly turn the trick into a bet. "In fact, if you can do it, I'll give you a ten-spot." At that they start to smile. "But if you can't, and I can do it, you owe me a ten-spot." Let the details of your proposition sink in. Ten-spot if they can, ten-spot if they can't but you can.

There's an art to persuading someone to take up a bet like this. You want to engage their minds on the problem, saying, "Anyone got any ideas how it can be done?" Once they are thinking about it, it is only a short step to them thinking about the possibility of winning your ten-spot. They ignore the fact that they might lose theirs.

"And I'll give you two attempts to do it, because it is tricky. Ten bucks says you can't. Ten bucks says I can." It won't be long before you smell the sweet scent of cash in the air as one in the increasingly curious crowd opens his wallet, pulls out a crisp bill and, unbeknownst to them, bids it farewell.

THE CATCH

This is a great trick. It's another stunt that's worth a ten-spot because everyone who sees it will be sure to try it on some other dumb-ass.

Most people, when confronted with this problem, will think back to that old stunt in which the juggler swipes away a tray and makes four eggs land in four glasses. That's good, because this trick doesn't work like that. They're not allowed to touch the coaster, and even if they slapped the edge of the table really hard, all they'd end up with for their trouble is a sore hand; the coin would end up anywhere but in the glass.

The secret to this little scam is a short sharp blast of air that you direct at the underside of the coaster. You will have to kneel down to do this and the glass should be positioned near the edge of the table. Blow upwards with a short sharp blast at the underside of the coaster and glass. The result is that the coaster flies away taking the cigarette with it and the coin drops straight down into the glass.

One of the reasons this works so well is that anyone who has spent the entire evening knocking back pints has usually got very little chance of being able to blow out enough air in a short blast to flip over that coaster – it's like asking them to blow into a Breathalyzer without using the tube.

Make sure you've practiced this a few times before trying it in front of your peers. And don't be surprised if the man handing over the tenner buys you a drink as well. As I said before, it's a damn good trick.

14 STICKS AND STONES

THE HOOK

"Sticks and stones may break my bones but words will never hurt me." I bet you've heard that said a few times. Well, it's about time to find out if the cliché is true with this next bet. Let me just say, it might be a good idea to have a few of your pals standing close by when you attempt to pull this one off.

Picking on the smallest guy in the group you say, "You're not looking too good today, Kevin." He'll wonder what you mean. "You just look a bit run down, that's all. A bit on the weak side. You feeling all right?"

As you are feeding him the bait, place a glass tumbler upside down on the table. And on it, place a matchbox. Take two of the matches out and hand these to Kevin.

"In fact, you look so weak that I bet that you can't even take these two matches and lift that matchbox from the top of the tumbler."

Having seen you in action before, Kevin will be a little suspicious. You lift the matchbox away and then drop it back down, saying, "It's not glued in place or anything."

"Look, take a matchstick in each hand. Now I bet you a ten-spot that using those matchsticks, you can't lift that matchbox from the top of the tumbler within the next twenty seconds."

Say it again if you have to. Kevin might not be a professional bodybuilder but he's sure that even he can manage this one. "Are you ready? I'm going to give you twenty seconds and before the time is up you have to lift the matchbox from the top of the tumbler. Do we have a deal?"

Of course you have a deal. What's more, Kevin does manage to lift the matchbox using the two matchsticks and within your twenty second time limit. Unfortunately, as he'll soon find out, it isn't enough to win the bet. He should, as he's about to discover, have payed a bit more attention in class.

THE CATCH

Alas for poor Kevin the con is all in the wording. You bet him that he couldn't lift the matchbox from the top of the tumbler. He can't because the tumbler is upside down and the matchbox is actually resting on the bottom, not the top. This might sound stupid but as anyone who has argued with his insurer will know, words are very important when it comes to making a contract. And, as with this stunt, it's always the sucker who loses.

The time limit you set on the bet ensures that the sucker doesn't have too long to think about it, and it also acts as a red herring. He will be busy trying to grab the matchbox between the matchsticks as you count him down from twenty to one. Get everybody to join in – that way, at the conclusion, everyone seems to be on your side and he's slightly less likely to make a fuss.

Maybe next time Kevin will pay more attention to what you say. And he'll definitely be checking those insurance policies when he gets home.

⓯ DOWN IN ONE

THE HOOK

They've seen it on television, they've seen it on vacation, and they've probably even seen it down at their local bar. Sometime sooner or later every Tough Guy will try downing a drink in one go, whether it's a pint of lager, a mug of ale, or a jug of lousy Sangria. Why does this phenomenon exist? So that you can pull this scam, that's why.

First, set out your stall, asking Bob the Belly, who you know has a throat like an open drain, whether he could down his pint all at once. No doubt he will boast of the many fine times he's had impressing the lucky señoritas of Cancun by doing just that. His mother must be so proud.

Having confirmed your character assessment, you issue the challenge: "I bet you couldn't drink a pint in thirty seconds." Thirty seconds? He will laugh at such a thought. And within less time than it takes to burp, he has placed a grubby ten-dollar bill on the table and is looking for you to do the same.

You draw in some spectators to see fair play, and one of them acts as timekeeper. Bob orders a fresh pint and feels so confident that he persuades the bartender to fill it to the very brim. No head.

"Ready, set, go!" The bellymeister lifts the pint, tilts it to a well-practiced angle, and proceeds to drain the contents. He's good. He's very good – a fact that you'll depend upon.

The empty glass is slammed against the bar, a pudgy hand wipes across thick wet lips, and he asks, "How'd I do?"

"You did fine," says the man with the watch. "Ten seconds dead." Bob is about to reach for the money but he is too late. You are already placing it into your wallet. And the wide-eyed expression on your victim demands an explanation.

THE CATCH

The Belly has been defeated by something he never quite mastered. Words, of the unslurred variety. The bet, as you remind him, was "to drink the pint in thirty seconds." Unfortunately for him, he did it in ten. Not quite the same thing.

Let his protests fall on deaf ears. Possession is nine-tenths of the law: you might not technically have a legal background but you watched a hell of a lot of *Judge Judy* on daytime TV when you were between jobs.

The very best defense you have for shady bets is to immediately give the sucker a chance to win his money back with another proposition. For some bizarre reason this tends to satisfy honor. It will be equally dubious but he doesn't need to know that. The notion that he might lose a second time hardly enters into it. But then maybe that's not surprising. After all, he didn't think he'd lose the first time around either.

16 BOTTLE OPENER

THE HOOK

If you managed to get away with a verbal con of the kind used in *Down in One* then here's one that could earn you a bottle of champagne.

It depends on a friendly bartender, a gullible victim, and some slick talking. Bob the Belly will see a possibility for revenge when you make the following offer, "I bet I can take a drink out of a bottle of champagne without opening it."

"What bottle of champagne?" asks Bob.

"The one you're going to pay for if I succeed," you reply. You also add that if you fail, the champagne is on you.

Bob will still be licking his wounds from the last bet, but he'll ask all the right questions. Are you really not going to open it? Not going to break the neck off the bottle or drill a hole through its side? Don't get into too many details if you can help it. Just repeat the challenge, "I promise I'll take a drink from the bottle without opening it, breaking the seal, removing the cork, or damaging the bottle in any way." Sounds fair enough and with a bit of prodding, he'll eventually accept the bet.

As soon as he does, you ask the bartender to loan you a bottle of champagne. This shouldn't be too difficult because he knows that at the end of the bet one or the other of you will be paying for it. As usual, however, it won't be you.

THE CATCH

So how do you take a drink from a sealed bottle of champagne without opening it first? Once again words come to your rescue and lure the unwary into the pit of poverty.

When you get the bottle of champagne, look it over very carefully. This is just to build the tension because everyone there will be wondering how on earth you can rise to this challenge. Pick at the top a little, just enough to get Bob to protest. Then look at the label. Apparently satisfied, you remind everyone of the challenge. "I said I'd take a drink out of this bottle without opening it. And if I can, Bobby here has promised to pay for the champagne. Isn't that right, Roberto?" He will admit that it is, thereby sealing the deal and his fate before witnesses.

As soon as he does that, you pick up your pint from the bar and turn the champagne bottle upside-down. You'll notice that, unlike most beer and wine bottles, there is a small concave hollow in its base. Pour some of your pint into this, put the rest of the drink down and then take a swig from the bottom of the bottle. You've met the challenge of taking a drink from the bottle without opening it. You never did say that you would be drinking champagne from it. But you will now.

⑰ FILL HER UP

THE HOOK

It's not that I don't like paying for drinks. It's just that if I can see a way of getting them for free, I have an irresistible urge to pull a scam. Paul Newman summed it up in the movie, *The Color of Money*: "A dollar won is twice as sweet as a dollar earned." Ain't that the truth.

Common sense tells you that it is not always possible to drink for free but that doesn't mean you need to pay full price either. Take the following; it won't make you a fortune but it will get you drinks at bargain prices.

The proposition is best used early in the evening. That way you establish a pattern and are free to try it on everyone who comes your way. In fact, you'll find that those whom you've already unashamedly hustled positively encourage you to pull it on their friends. No one wants to be singled out as stupid and so they find comfort in the humiliation of their peers.

Here is the wager. When your friends arrive, after they've bought their drinks, single one of them out and say, "I bet you that I can drink your drink, snap my fingers, and make it instantly reappear in your glass. And I will swallow it – no spitting it out or any tricks like that, I promise! In fact you can even hold the empty glass. And to make it even more difficult, place this coaster over the top and hold it down tight so that nothing can get inside."

No one who knows you will want to bet with you, not after you've been working all the stunts in this book. But your friend will still be intrigued. He'll definitely want to see this trick. A glass magically refilling itself? Sounds like the miracle he's always dreamed of. So you make it easy for him to take the wager by saying, "It's just for fun. Say fifty cents?"

Well, fifty cents isn't much to lose and you've just got yourself a deal. But how will you make the trick work?

THE CATCH

The answer is that you don't. There is no easy way that you can make a drink reappear in the glass while he's holding it. And you're not going to waste time trying to figure out how you could do it either.

What you are going to do is savor his drink when you take it. And when it fails to reappear in the glass, you hand him your fifty cents. It will be the cheapest drink you'll buy all evening but not the only one because you can pull the same scam on every friend of his that arrives at the bar.

18 CAP IN HAND

THE HOOK

Not everyone will appreciate your wit and verbal dexterity. The thought that you cheated them out of their cash or a drink using simply a few choice phrases could be considered a bit underhanded. People like Bob the Belly would prefer something more honest. Arm wrestling over broken glass for instance. It's wise therefore to play to what they imagine are their strengths. In this case you challenge Bob to come outside and sort it out man to man. Well, almost.

What you actually say is, "I bet I can throw a bottle cap farther than you. Much farther. Ten bucks says I can." And as a taster of your Olympian skills you pick up a bottle cap and skim it across the bar.

Like the bartender, Bob is not impressed. He's a member of the neighborhood football team; when he's not knocking back beer he's chasing and hugging other big men with odd-shaped balls.

Pick up another bottle cap and bend it between your fingers, as an open exhibition of brute force. And challenge him again. "What do you say? Ten bucks says I can throw a bottle cap farther than you can. Are you coming outside or what?"

The thought that everyone might think him too chicken to step outside with you is enough to goad him into action again, and another portrait of Alex Hamilton is teased from his wallet. Five minutes later you are both standing in the parking lot with a handful of bottle caps. Each of you is allowed to make a couple of practice throws but it's the third one that will count. Whoever throws their bottle cap farthest wins the contest – that much is fair.

Bob gives it his best shot – the wind blows the cap in a curve but it's a good throw all the same. Seeing this you take off your jacket and start to get serious. You take a short run and then fling your bottle cap into the air. It leaves your hand with amazing speed, sailing out of the parking lot, over the road, and off into the distance. There's no doubt who the winner is.

THE CATCH

This stunt is a version of a favorite of that great American gambler Titanic Thompson, only he did it with walnuts rather than beer bottle caps. He had prepared his walnut beforehand by filling it full of lead shot. The extra weight meant that he could outdistance even a professional sportsman when it came to the throw.

You use the same swindle, but insert a coin into the bottle cap before you throw it. The coin should be as close to the internal diameter of the bottle cap as possible; with some you will be able to just wedge them in place, with others you might need to bend over opposite sides of the cap slightly to grip them. The added weight gives your cap extra momentum, and even with moderate strength you should be able to throw yours considerably farther than your opponent. Save this one for the evening. That way no one is likely to find your weighted bottle cap in the dark.

⑲ LOT OF BOTTLE

THE HOOK

It was the shape of the bottle that made the bet in *Bottle Opener* possible and so it is with this next proposition. It requires three of the original-style Coca-Cola bottles.

You arrange the bottles so that one of them is lying on the table trapped by its middle between the other two.

Then you take a match and lodge it between the bottles as shown. Although the bottles hold the match in place, the slightest shifting of them will cause the match to fall. When it's set up, you make your bet.

"I'll give ten bucks to anyone who can free the center bottle without the match falling. Problem is that you can't touch either of the other bottles, only the center one. And you can't touch the match. Ten bucks says it can be done. Any takers?"

Let your prospective suckers study the puzzle from all angles but don't let them touch anything until they've taken your bet. Only he who pays, plays.

Best of all, you will give the challenger two attempts to solve it.

THE CATCH

At first glance it looks impossible. The middle bottle is held locked between the other two. Those who attempt the challenge usually try to move the bottle upwards towards the neck and free it where the gap is widest. But moving the bottle is almost sure to make the match fall. It really doesn't matter whether they have two or three attempts to solve the puzzle; it just won't work that way.

The solution is ingenious and you should only reveal it when you are sure the money is going to be paid over. You pick up the matchbox from which you took the match, and take out a second matchstick. Strike it and use it to set light to the head of the first matchstick. It will flare up immediately and weld itself to the bottle. You can now simply pull the middle bottle free. The outer bottles will separate but the matchstick will not fall.

20 RETURN TO LENDER

THE HOOK

This particular scam became popular with conmen in bars all over the United States around forty years ago.

This works best with a large crowd. First you befriend one of the bar staff and ask if you can borrow a ten- or twenty-dollar bill from the cash register, offering to show them an amazing trick. Have them sign the bill – "So that you'd recognize it if you ever saw it again" – and then fold it up into eighths. Place the note under a napkin or bar towel and let several people reach under and confirm that it is still there. It is.

Now for the magic. You flick the napkin open and, to everyone's amazement, the bill has disappeared. Completely gone. It's not up your sleeves, in the napkin, or in your hand. It's gone. Forever.

Well, you could bring it back if you wanted to. And that's when you turn the trick into a bet. "You've just lost ten bucks from the register. Is it worth a free drink to get it back? Let's say I make that same ten bucks reappear inside the cash register. Would that be a good trick? Would it be worth a drink?"

Of course it would. Now it's just a matter of getting the bartender to shout the magic words "Gribbity gree" as loud as he possibly can. And believe me, if he wants to get the money back, he will shout anything you tell him to. Personally, I make him stand on the bar, put one finger in his ear, and roll up a pant leg as well. But that's the sort of person I am.

Then, lo and behold, he's asked to open up the till and there inside is the bill for everyone to see, complete with his signature. What a trick! What a scam, actually.

THE CATCH

This is a racket from start to finish. First you need a buddy to act as a stooge. He is the last person to feel the bill under the napkin. He doesn't just feel it, he also secretly takes it from you and palms it away. If no one knows he's in on the scam, his actions won't be suspected.

While the attention is on you and the ritual humiliation of the bartender, your friend casually wanders away to the other end of the bar, taking the bill with him. He then asks one of the other bar staff for change for the cigarette machine, and that's the simple but sneaky way that the signed bill ends up back in the register and you end up with a free drink.

As I said before, this trick was used by conmen to swindle bars out of money – they made their profit from the change that is handed over to the stooge. Of course you wouldn't be that dishonest and neither would I – we'd hand the cash back afterwards. Wouldn't we?

A far more more honest and satisfying way of making a few bucks on top of your free drink is to make a side bet with someone beforehand: "A tenner says by the end of the evening that bartender will be up on the bar shouting 'Gribbity gree' with a finger in one ear and his pant leg rolled up."

TWO

TIPPED OFF

"A FOOL AND HIS MONEY WERE
LUCKY TO GET TOGETHER IN
THE FIRST PLACE."
— ANONYMOUS

THE HOOK

It's been a wonderful meal. And your buddy's been good company. Haven't seen him for ages. But this joint is a bit on the pricey side and you wonder why he picked such an elegant restaurant. It's as if along with his new promotion he's become a bit showy. Well, if he can afford his half of the meal, he can afford yours too.

The check arrives. It's got more numbers on it than a lottery ticket.

"Tell you what, let's toss for it," you say. He agrees and you take out a coin and flip it into the air.

By the time the coin lands, there's a good chance you might be eating for free. But the main thing is there's absolutely no chance that you will be paying for both meals.

THE CATCH

In the old days, a double-headed coin would have done the trick. But most people are wise to that one.

What they probably haven't seen is a coin that has been nicked at the edge with a knife on the tail side so that a tiny burr is projecting.

That's the coin you are using for the bet.

Timing is important on this one so listen up. Take out the coin as though at random from a handful of change as you say, "Tell you what, let's toss for it." As you already have a coin to hand, he won't offer to supply one himself. Toss the coin up in the air in time-honored tradition, catch it, and slap it on the back of your hand.

"Heads or tails?" you ask. While he thinks

about it, you press the coin against the back of your hand and slide it slightly. If it is heads up, you will feel the tiny projection on the tail side prick your skin. If it is tails up, you won't feel anything. In other words, you now know which call will be right.

If he calls incorrectly, uncover the coin and show him. You've just eaten for free.

If he calls correctly, you can do one of two things depending on how cocky you are feeling. Either smile and say, "No, I can't do it. I was going to trick you, but I can't take your money! We'll split the check," as you put the coin away *without ever looking at it*. He'll think you've just been joking all along.

Or, if you're like me, you'll just flip the coin over towards him with your thumb as you lift your hand away. It's actually very easy to do. Remember, he has no idea that you already know which way up the coin is.

So there you have it. Play the game almost fair and you'll dine for free half the time. Use the thumb swindle and you'll never pay for a meal again. Can't be fairer than that, can you?

㉒ IT'S A DATE

THE HOOK

"There's no point tossing a coin and calling heads or tails is there? There'd be a fifty-fifty chance I'd win, even if I didn't cheat." At least you're vaguely honest with your fellow diner as you make yet another attempt at a free meal. "Let me give you some real odds. Take out any coin from your pocket. Don't look at it and place it on the table. Cover it with your hand so that I can't see it."

"Now then," you say, "I'm prepared to bet you the cost of lunch that I can guess the date. Keep the coin covered. You can't let me see it. In fact, if you think I've already seen it, take out another coin and put it on the table."

This bet is definitely too good to refuse. The sucker's hand is on the coin. He knows that you don't even know what the coin is so how can you possibly guess the date? Ah, but you can. And that's why you won't be buying lunch.

THE CATCH

If your victim had drank less he might have listened more carefully. You never said that you'd tell him the date on the coin. What you said was that you would tell him the date. And so you do – today's date!

The bet can be played as a competition. You invite the sucker to take out a coin and cover it. You then say, "Whoever guesses closest to the correct date, gets a free lunch. The other one wins the coin and adds it to the money he'll need to pay the check." No matter what he calls, you once again call out today's date – leaving him with a hefty check.

There's one more tip that might occasionally come in handy in situations like this. As you can imagine, it can sometimes be difficult to get someone to pay out when you've just swindled them in such a basic way. But, if the sucker is a real man, one thing's for sure: he's unlikely to want to look like a bad loser in front of the waitress or lady bartender he's been ogling all night. So get her to hold your credit cards or cash until the bet's been settled. Having spent the entire meal drooling over her every move, he'll do anything to avoid looking like a cheapskate.

TIME IS MONEY

THE HOOK

The average sucker's powers of observation are not at their best after a wine-soaked meal. Which is just as well, because this bet depends on that fact.

You begin by asking your dining companion about his watch; how long has he had it, where did he buy it, how much did it cost him? General questions of no particular significance it might seem. Then you make the following proposition: "I'm going to ask you three questions about your watch. They are easy questions. If you get them all right, I'll buy dinner. If you get any of them wrong, dinner's on you. Now before we start, let me say that the questions are really very simple. So easy that if you don't agree that you should know the answers, we'll call the whole bet off."

If he decides to take the bet – and having answered your first questions without any problem he'd be hard pressed not to - then you've just enjoyed that meal for free.

THE CATCH

It is amazing how many times this scam works. People are amazingly poor observers when it comes to even the most personal of possessions and when put on the spot find themselves unable to recall even the simplest details. The only restriction with this wager is that you can only use it with victims who are wearing an analog watch as opposed to a digital one. Well, unless they are completely trashed, but where's the challenge in that?

Here are the questions:

 Without looking, does your watch have a second hand? More than likely he will get this one right. Let him answer and then move on to the next question.

 Again without looking, does your watch have a number 6 on it? This is quite tricky. He probably won't remember whether the watch has Roman or Arabic numerals. And many watches don't have any numbers at all; just lines at the 3, 6, 9, and 12 hour positions, if anything at all. When he's answered, ask him to check his watch and let you know if he was correct.

 Finally, and this is the killer, ask him what time it is – without looking at his watch again. Despite the fact that he just looked at it a few seconds ago, the chances are that he never noted the time.

If you're in any doubt about whether that's likely to be the case, try asking someone the time and then ask them the same question again just moments later and see whether or not they can answer you correctly without having another look.

WORTH A PACKET

THE HOOK

Ever got caught by one of those fake auctions where they promise to sell you a television, a DVD player, and a dishwasher, all for five bucks, and when you get back home you find that what you've actually bought is a set of plastic wrenches? Well, you'll find the same auction fever at work here.

It begins simply enough. You ask one of your dining compadres for twenty bucks, enough to cover your share of the meal you've just had. If he has any sense, he'll say no. But you persuade him to play your game by offering up twenty bucks of your own. Fold it up and stick it in an empty cigarette pack. Having put your own money down, ask for his, saying, "Come on, twenty bucks, I'm about to make you an offer you can't refuse."

Take his twenty, fold it up, and put it in the cigarette pack with yours. Hold the box up and give it a shake, saying, "There's forty bucks inside here. Have I taken anything out of the pack since we began?" He'll have to agree that you haven't. You've been careful to let him see your hands empty all the time you've been handling the money.

"In that case, would you give me fifty bucks for this pack and its contents?" Of course he wouldn't. "How about forty?" Still not exactly a bargain; all he'd be gaining is the cigarette pack. "Well how about if I offered to sell you the lot for thirty bucks?" He considers the offer and eventually agrees. Who wouldn't?

THE CATCH

The truth is that if he gives you thirty bucks for the forty in the cig pack, he's actually buying back twenty bucks of his own, therefore losing out to the tune of ten smackers…think about it.

NUMBERS UP

THE HOOK

One of the secrets of a good bet is luring the victim into a situation that makes it comfortable for him to risk his money. That means getting the money from his wallet and onto the table without arousing suspicion. So it's always good to start with a puzzle or a bit of trivia. For instance:

"Do you know what the most commonly used letter in the English language is?" He might or might not, but the answer, as you inform him, is the letter *e*. Fascinating. Now you take it one stage further. "Do you know what the most commonly used digits from zero to nine are?"

Let him guess three digits and whatever he says agree with him. "Two, five, and seven? That's absolutely right. That's amazing; you've obviously got a lucky streak. In fact I bet that if you took out a ten-dollar bill from your wallet, you'd find at least two of these digits in the serial number."

Take out a ten-spot of your own, and place it on the table, saying, "And if there isn't, you can have my ten. On the other hand, if there is, I get to keep yours."

THE CATCH

There are eight digits in the serial number on a bill, any of which could obviously be one of the numbers that your sucker calls. They can choose any three digits so long as they are different. The odds are heavily in your favor

on this one but you will still sometimes lose, so on that basis you might want
to play it with everyone you meet. Who needs friends anyway?

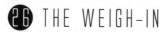# 26 THE WEIGH-IN

THE HOOK

"I'm going to ask you some simple questions. If you manage to get them all
right, I'll pay for lunch. If you get one wrong, you pay for lunch."

It is, of course, another one of your famous "can't lose" propositions. And
it all appears to be done purely in the name of fun. (Of course it does.) As
you issue the challenge, you arrange several small objects from your
pockets on the table. You need a packet of cigarettes (preferably empty or
close to it), a small coin, and a cigarette lighter. Line them up in a row just
in front of the sucker.

"Are you ready?" You don't wait to see whether he wants to play or not –
that should never be an option. It is entirely up to him to say no. By not
saying anything, he becomes party to the bet – it's as good as a contract –
especially if you have other people at the table watching what you are doing.
Never underestimate the power of peer pressure.

"Okay, now listen carefully. I'm going to ask you to pick up two objects at
a time. Then I'll ask you a question about them. And there will be three
questions in all. Understand?"

His "yes" to understanding what the bet is about will be taken by everyone
else to also be a "yes" to accepting the bet itself, which you now repeat in
case anyone is in any doubt. "If you get all three questions right, I'll pay for
your meal. If you get one wrong, you pay for mine. Okay?" His grunt can also
be taken as acknowledgment of his willing participation.

And then you go straight into the questions. Need I say that he won't get
them all correct?

THE CATCH

The objects on the table are not as randomly chosen as they appear. For the first question you point to the pack of cigarettes and the coin and ask him to pick them up, one in each hand. Then you say, "Which is the biggest one?"

He'll say the pack of cigarettes, which is obviously the right answer, and you tell him to put them down. Note that you only ever point to the objects. You never ever name them.

Now, point to the cigarette packet and the lighter and ask him to pick them up. Ask him, "Which one is the heavier?" He'll say it is the cigarette lighter. Correct again. Ask him to put them down.

Finally, get him to pick up the coin in one hand and the cigarette lighter in the other and ask him, "Which is the lighter?" Amazing as it may seem, he will nominate the coin because he has been thinking in terms of size and weight. To your own selfish and devious ends you point to the cigarette lighter and say, "No, that's the lighter; that's the coin."

Another free lunch to you.

COINING IT IN

THE HOOK

It's a well know fact that after a few drinks the brain's powers of observation and logic go into a steady decline. Perversely, though, and fortunately for us, El Vino convinces even the most sensible that his powers of perception have been enhanced beyond measure.

The following bet exploits your sucker's alcohol-induced infallibility. Which is just as well because you've been reduced to raiding the piggy bank for this one. You will need a lot of coins, all the same value. Let's assume that your total worth at this point in time can be summed up with a handful of quarters.

Arrange them on the table in small piles. The first pile consists of a single coin. The second pile has five coins. The third nine coins, the fourth twelve coins, and the fifth fifteen coins. Five piles of coins, arranged in a row as shown.

Keep one coin on display as you make your wager. "Which of these piles of coins do you think is as high as the coin is wide?"

You might have to speak slowly to make sure you are understood. So say it again if you have to, expanding on the premise so that it is clear even to the dullest. "Which pile of coins is the same height as this coin is wide?" Hold up the coin for him to see and then place it away in your pocket.

To give his choice an edge, you wager the price of the meal on him being unable to choose the right pile. It seems a simple bet but more often than not, your victim will be wrong.

THE CATCH

This is a cunning optical illusion and you will need to try it with some coins to fully appreciate how effective it is. In the case of the quarters, most people will pick the fourth pile of coins. Twelve coins seem more than ample to equal the diameter of a quarter. But they'd be wrong. The correct pile is the last one containing fifteen coins and you prove this by taking out another quarter and standing it on end beside it.

The trick works with any coin, but you'll need to vary the number of coins accordingly. Just make sure that you leave enough space between the piles to further confuse the eye.

28 MATCH POINT

THE HOOK

There's nothing like a friendly after-dinner game to sort out who should pay the check. And that's what this is; nothing like a friendly game.

You take out a box of matches, which you just happen to have with you, and tip the contents into an ashtray. The game is simple. You and the fall guy each take a number of matches from the ashtray alternately. Whoever takes the last match is the winner. The loser buys lunch.

There is only one rule: each time you reach into the ashtray you can only take up to three matches. One, two, or three, that's it. But because the sucker hasn't played this game before, you give him the advantage of taking the first turn — you're a charitable kind of guy.

He reaches in and takes some matches. You do the same. And you continue this until one of you wins the game by taking the last match from the ashtray. Naturally, it will be you.

THE CATCH

The game is rigged from the start. You know exactly how many matches are in the matchbox. It doesn't have to be any precise number though, as long as it is divisible by four. I find that thirty-two or thirty-six matches make for a good game.

Let the sucker take the first turn and watch how many matches he takes. Then, when you take your turn, take enough matches to make his number up to four. For example, if he takes one match, you take three. If he takes two matches, you also take two. Every time he takes matches you take enough to make it up to the magical number four.

If you are mathematically minded, you can probably see where this is leading. At the end of the game there will be four matches left in the ashtray, but since he can only take up to three matches, it leaves you with the last one. And it leaves him with the lunch bill.

Incidentally, there's an additional twist on this. Start by demonstrating the game, telling him that the object is for each of you to remove up to three matches at a time. Once he understands that, ask him whether he would like to take the first or the second turn. If he chooses to go first, you announce that whoever takes the last match is the winner. If he chooses to go second, tell him that whoever takes the last match is the loser. Either way, using the same principle as above, you can always maneuver him into a losing position.

29 GAME, SET, AND MATCH

THE HOOK

Believe it or not, quite often you can earn yourself a little extra cash by simply explaining how you conned your victim in the first place. *Match Point* is a good example. Having won the bet and ensured that the loser paid the bill, you can later offer to share the secret of your success, for a price. It may be a drink at the bar or much more. It all depends on how desperate your victim is to know and how good your negotiating skills are.

You set the price, then you explain the trick — when he took his turn you observed the number of matches he removed and simply did a little addition to work out how many matches you should take. Pour some matches into the ashtray and let him practice a little. He will soon get the hang of it. And when he has, you make him another little wager. In fact you confess to feeling a bit guilty that you swindled a good lunch out of him.

"How about we play a game for a ten-spot? This time I'll go first."

Like a lamb at a butchers convention, he quickly agrees and the game begins. And yet, although he follows your strategy exactly, he still manages to lose. Too bad, because as soon as you've got your hands on his tenner, you suddenly remember a previous appointment. Got to run.

THE CATCH

Turning a crooked game into an even more crooked game is a favorite ruse of professional cheats. There is no one as easily deceived as someone who's got his heart set on cheating someone else. So watch out.

The trick is simple but needs to be executed with an air of nonchalance. You take the first turn and play the strategy you have outlined. You proceed in this way until about half the matches have been taken. Next time it is your turn, take out some matches and place them on the table. However, don't place them all on the table. Keep just one hidden in your fingers. Next time you take your turn, drop the hidden match into the ashtray as you dip into it. The sucker won't spot this. Take your turn as usual and let him count how many matches you have removed.

Because of the extra match, the victim's entire strategy has been spoiled. Instead of four matches in the ashtray near the end of the game, there will be five. And if you play the finish correctly, you can always leave him with the last match and walk away with his ten-spot.

Another good way to use this swindle is to persuade him to use it on one of your buddies. What he doesn't realize is that your pal also knows about secretly putting a match back into the ashtray.

My own personal tactic is to offer to hold the money while the two of them play. Halfway through I'm "unexpectedly" called to the phone – that way I can't be held responsible if our chump messes up and loses.

You can split the winnings with your buddy later.

THE HOOK

In this scam you don't just win one meal, you win two. Imagine the scene; you and a couple of buddies, Bob and Dave, out for burritos, ordering without bothering to look at the prices on the menu because you know that although a hefty check will be coming your way, you won't be paying it. Not that you are stingy – much. Divided between the three of you, it wouldn't break the bank, but how much better if Dave, who quite frankly came along uninvited and you've never liked him anyway, was to pay all of it?

Before the bill arrives, and therefore before Dave can discover the true scale of his potential losses, you explain a little dinner ritual that you and Bob have had for years. Rather than deal with all that complicated long division and trying to figure out who had what, you just toss a match and whoever loses pays the bill. You demonstrate by taking the book of matches from the ashtray and tearing one out. You mark one side of the match with an X. The other side is marked with a O. Then you toss the match and let it fall on the table. It is just a variation on tossing a coin and calling heads or tails.

Since Dave has made it a trio, this complicates things a bit. Or so you say. Then you have an idea.

"I'll tell you what, Dave, it's your first time here, so we'll let you off easy. If it comes down X side up, I'll pay. If it comes down O side up, Bob pays. And if it lands on its edge, you pay!"

Give a laugh as you make the bet, as if the chances of a paper match landing on its edge were more remote than winning the lottery without buying a ticket. Bob plays the innocent, laughs too, and says, "Why not?" forcing Dave to agree – after all, it looks like he's in for a free meal. However, as you've probably learned by now, things are not quite as they seem and it'll be a long time before Davey boy cramps your style again.

THE CATCH

Not much to explain on this one. It takes a lot of practice to toss a paper match so that it lands on its edge, but you can help it out by bending it into an "L" shape just before you throw it.

As you swing your hand upwards to make the toss, lay the match across

your fingers and push against its centre with your thumbnail. It will crease instantly and, much to Dave's surprise and irritation, will come down to land on its edge.

FOUR PLAY

THE HOOK

A book of matches offers a surprising number of possibilities for extracting cash from the unwary. Here's one of my favorites. I like it because there's no chance of the sucker deciding not to play. The money is gone before he even suspects that he's put it at risk.

It's Friday night, much alcohol has been consumed, and dinner was great. If only it didn't cost so much. Time to start defraying your expenses by picking out a likely looking individual and involving him in a little party game. Tell him you'll show him a trick and ask him for the loan of a tenner. People never loan money to strangers but they seem happy to hand it and other valuables freely to magicians knowing full well that it will come to harm. It's something I've never understood, but I'm grateful that they do.

Place the ten-spot in the middle of the table. Make a big deal of straightening the bill out so that it's absolutely flat. And if you can't iron all the wrinkles out of it, ask for a crisper bill. The idea is to take the victim's mind far away from any thought that he might be about to lose his money. Bear in mind that if you are using the scams in this book, your reputation might well have preceded you. Some people are going to be cautious about handing over their hard-earned cash.

Take out a matchbook, tear out four matches, and arrange them around the note, one on each of the four sides. Again, make a big deal of setting the matches exactly parallel with the sides of the note. This is all bluff and bluster and has nothing to do with the scam.

With everything set, say, "I bet you a buck that you won't answer 'four matches' to every question I ask. And I'm going to ask four questions only, one for each match."

A buck isn't much to lose and only a dick wouldn't play along. On the other hand, he'll regret it the moment he does.

THE CATCH

These are the questions you ask: "What is your name?" He will answer, "Four matches," and you give him one of the matches from the table.

"Where do you live?" Again he answers, "Four matches," and you give him another one.

"What's this on the table?" You say, pointing to the ten-spot. He answers as before and gets his third match in return.

"What will you take for this ten-spot?" And this is crunch time. If he isn't thinking (and most people aren't), he will say, "Four matches," at which point you hand him the fourth match and pocket the ten-spot.

And if he doesn't fall for that, you've still won the buck from your original bet. All you have to do now is go find nine other schmucks.

32 CUP WINNER

THE HOOK

You've got to know what you are doing when you're working this one, but done casually it can be a winner. You hand a matchbook to your sucker and ask him to take out a bunch of matches, tear them in half, and drop them into an empty coffee cup. You are doing the same with a second book of matches: tearing some matches out, breaking them in half, and dropping them into the same cup. After you've done this with a dozen or so matches, put your matchbook aside and ask him to do the same. So far, so fair.

No one knows how many bits of match are in the cup and so it seems like a reasonable bet when you propose that each of you alternately reach in and take out a piece until the cup is empty. Whoever takes the last piece pays for the meal. The proposition is anything but reasonable. Even though you have no idea how many matches are in the cup, you're certain that you'll win.

THE CATCH

No matter how many matches are torn from the matchbooks, there will always be an even number of pieces in the cup because you broke them all into two. So if you take your turn first, your victim will always be left with the last piece.

In the cold light of day the ruse seems absurd, but in my experience people rarely think that clearly the night before, especially if they are having a good time. Which they will be until the check arrives.

If you're feeling generous, you can offer your opponent a "rematch," this time offering to let him take the first piece from the cup. Of course, what he doesn't know is that when you tore your matches in half you didn't put all pieces in the cup. You secretly kept one back. With an odd number of pieces in play, once again he will lose.

33 MATCHBOX MONTE

THE HOOK

It's said that the best way to make a small fortune is to start with a big one. That's also true of anyone who's happy to throw their money at the monte men that work the streets of most major cities. Whether they are throwing around three cards and asking you to "find the lady" or manipulating three walnut shells and a pea, the outcome is always the same: you lose. But in this game you're the winner, because now you're playing the role of the monte man and your dinner companion plays the part of the sucker.

You ask the waiter for three boxes of matches and he obliges. You tip out the matches from the boxes so that they're all empty. Then, hiding them underneath the table, you refill one of them with matches. The question is which one?

You lay the three boxes in a row on the table, mix them around, and ask your compadre to point to whichever one he thinks contains the matches. If he has any sense, he will tell you that it's impossible to know – how could he? He's right, so you demonstrate which one it is by picking up one of the boxes and rattling it before putting it down again. "Okay, let's start again. I'm going to mix the boxes up and all you have to do is keep your eye on the one that's full."

. Slowly you mix the boxes up, moving them one at a time around the table. Then you ask him again which box contains the matches. He immediately points to one and this time he's correct. Now you turn up the heat. "Good. Let's play it again and this time, if you get the right box, I'll pay for the meal. But if you guess wrong, dinner's on you, okay?"

He thinks the game is easy, which is a shame because as soon as the game turns into a bet he has absolutely no chance of picking out the right box.

THE CATCH

What your friend across the table doesn't know is that you have a fourth matchbox hidden up your right sleeve. It contains a few matches and is held against your arm by an elastic band. You hid it there on your last visit to the john.

When you load matches into one of the boxes, make sure you know which one it is. You might want to mark it by running your thumbnail across the top. This is because the first part of the game is played fairly. You mix the boxes up and ask the sucker to guess which one contains the matches. As he didn't see which box you put them into, he'll probably complain about how unfair the game is. That's when you pick up one of the empty matchboxes with the right hand and give it a shake. He'll hear the matches rattling in the box strapped to your forearm and will assume that the empty box in your hand is actually full. Put this box down on the table and begin the second phase of the game.

Move the boxes around slowly, making sure that the sucker is following the empty matchbox. That's the box he'll point to at the finish. Again, pick it up with the right hand and give it a quick shake. He hears the matches rattle around and congratulates himself on his powers of observation.

Having got him interested you make the wager and mix the boxes around for the third time. The loser is still following the empty box and at the end of the game will be absolutely amazed when he finds that his wallet is just as empty.

 DROPPING THE CHARGES

THE HOOK

"Do you believe in hypnotism?" you ask the sucker. "Because I bet I can hypnotize you. I'm sure I can. You look the type." Now no one likes to look like "the type," so they'll ask what you mean. "You look suggestible," you reply. "In fact, I'm prepared to bet dinner on it." The stage is set for a demonstration of bogus hypnosis that will hopefully land you a real meal.

THE CATCH

You show him what to do by placing your hands together palm to palm, as if in prayer. Rest your elbows on the table. Ask him to do as you do and follow your actions precisely. As he does, you tell him to spread out his fingers.

Next, tell him to bend his middle fingers inwards so that they cross. Finally, pick up the check, fold it and slide it between his extended third fingers.

So far he won't feel anything other than uncomfortable, but it's now that the bet really begins.

"You've got to keep your hands tight together. Keep hold of the check. Keep your middle fingers bent. That's important; you *really* don't want to

separate your hands. Keep your thumbs together. Understand?"

He'll understand. Now you start your hypnotic hocus pocus. "I want you to count backwards from ten to one, and as you count, the fingers of your hand will grow numb and will start to

lose their feeling. So much so that when I snap my fingers you won't be able to drop the check onto the table without moving your *other* fingers. That's the only way you will be able to drop the check. Are you ready?"

Get him to count slowly "ten, nine, eight, seven," and so on. When he gets to "one" snap your fingers and say, "The check is yours. The check is yours. The check *is* yours." He can shake his hands around as much as he likes but no matter how hard he tries he won't be able to release the check from between his fingers without pulling his hands apart or making some other digital adjustment. It has nothing to do with hypnosis though; it's just another top swindle. The check really is his, though.

A RIGHT HANDFUL

THE HOOK

"How about we arm wrestle for the meal? No, just kidding. Don't want to cause a scene." You are preparing the way for an interesting little wager. "Besides, you're bigger than me. Probably break my arm." You are in fact just basting the turkey a little before serving him up. "But I'm willing to bet you this. That there's something here, right now, that you can lift with your right hand but not with your left."

It sounds sketchy and you won't want to say this too loudly otherwise you'll get some very funny looks from the other tables. But you do want to get out of paying for this meal so you go over it again, quietly, "I can see that your left hand is a bit weak. So, as I say, I think there is something right here, in plain sight, that you can lift with your right hand but you'd have trouble holding in your left hand. In fact I'm so sure you that can't pick it up with your left hand that I'll bet the price of dinner on it."

Look at the array of objects on the table as you speak, implying that the object in question might be an empty wine bottle, a coffee cup, or a plate. And wait for curiosity to get the better of him.

THE CATCH

With the bet accepted you ask him to hold out both hands. Then you push his left hand upwards while holding his right hand, palm upwards, at table height. Repeat the wager, "I bet the price of dinner that there is something you can lift with your right hand but can't with your left," and then bring his right palm up to his left elbow.

He can lift his left elbow in his right hand, but he'll never be able to hold it with his left hand. Ignore the people on the other tables who are staring at you and your elbow-fondling friend; there are other restaurants you can go to next time.

CATCH OF THE DAY

THE HOOK

When you went to the fish restaurant, you never thought you'd end the meal with an angling competition, but that's what you do in this next scam.

The waiter brings over two glasses of water and floating in each of them is an ice cube. "Imagine that's a fish," you say, "and this is your line." The line is nothing more than a length of cotton thread, which you just happened to have with you. You snap it in two, take half yourself and hand the other half to the sucker.

"Here's the game." Describing it as a game takes the heat out of the situation. People like games; they're not so keen on cons. "You've got to use the thread to fish the ice out of the glass. First one to do it is the winner. You can't touch the glass, the water, or the ice. That's the rule."

What a wonderfully stupid game, thinks your friend. And just as he is thinking that, you add a rider to the rules, "Loser pays the check. Winner gets a free meal." Now this might seem a bit harsh so you pacify the sucker by adding, "But you have to pull the ice out of the glass in less than sixty seconds to win. Do you want to try first? You just lower the thread in like this."

You give a demonstration, and take your thread between your hands and lower the middle into the glass where you attempt, unsuccessfully, to loop it around the ice cube. It won't take long for your clever pal to figure out that this is quite a difficult game. And after he has given it a try himself, he'll have no doubt that it's impossible to get the ice out of the glass in under sixty seconds. And so, just as you'd intended, the bet is on and you've all but landed yourself a fish supper.

THE CATCH

A little trickery is used here. It's virtually impossible to drag the ice out of the glass using the thread. At least I've never managed to do it. Not without cheating.

The cheat consists of some salt, which you have hidden in your hand. Earlier in the meal, when the sucker wasn't looking, you grabbed the saltshaker and poured some of its contents into a small heap on your lap. You might have to sneak the top off to do this properly.

While he is practicing looping his thread, you lower your thread onto the ice in your glass.

Then secretly bring up a pinch of salt and drop it on top of the ice cube and thread. All this is done while your fellow fisherman is concentrating on his own fishing tackle. The salt melts the ice, which quickly refreezes around the thread, welding it to the cube. Pretend that you are practicing too for a while, then officially start the competition. All you have to do is pull on the thread carefully and you will be able to lift the ice cube right out of the water. He's been caught hook, line, and sinker.

THE HOOK

To do this one well, you've got to lead your sucker down the garden path and then bolt the gate behind you before he can figure out a way back.

You place two quarters on the table and a smaller coin, say a dime, between them. Then you set a pint glass of soda on top of it. The glass is full and there is a straw in it. Here's the setup.

"How long do you think it would take you to drink that glass of soda?" Doesn't really matter what he answers because you now tell him, "Well, here's a challenge. See that dime sitting under the glass? I bet I can get it from under the glass faster than you can. Now obviously you're probably thinking that the fastest way of getting the coin is to move the glass. Well, the rule is that you can't move the glass until it's empty. And you can't touch the glass or the coins either. So how fast do you think you can get the coin?"

Whatever he says, offer to bet him the meal that you can do it quicker. You even give him an opportunity to go first. And, if you've led him down the right garden path, he'll start drinking the soda through the straw so that he can then move the glass according to the rules. Time him on your watch, congratulate him, and then show that there's an even faster way.

THE CATCH

The trick is that drinking the pint of soda through a straw is not the quickest way to get at the coin. There is another way, although it only succeeds if you are working on a tablecloth.

The trick is to scratch at the tablecloth just to one side of the glass, between the two larger coins. Strangely, this sets the coin in motion and if you keep scratching it will slowly crawl towards you and out from under the glass. Easy, really. And you don't feel bloated afterward.

TOSS UP

THE HOOK

Here's one for the brave. It isn't a bet you'll win every time, but you'll certainly be ahead in the long run. It depends on the laws of probability, those unwritten rules that have caught many a gambler who thought he could fool Lady Luck.

Ask your sucker what the odds are of heads coming up if you toss a coin. He should answer fifty-fifty, which is correct. Then ask him how many times heads would come up if you tossed a coin ten times. Doesn't take a genius to figure out that the answer must be five.

"Well, that's interesting. Because I bet you that if you toss a coin ten times, you won't get five heads." Let him think about it, and then make him a wager he can't refuse.

THE CATCH

While he might toss five heads and five tails, he might also toss one head and nine tails, two heads and eight tails, three heads and — well, you get the idea. There are far more combinations possible in ten trials than the one he thinks most probable. The true situation is that the odds of anything other than five heads being tossed are five to two in your favor. Play this strategy over a long run and you should see a substantial profit.

39 IT'S A CORKER

THE HOOK

An empty wine bottle usually signals the end of an evening. But for you, it's the opening of a new gambit by which a little extra pocket money can be earned.

You take the cork that came out of the bottle and push it back inside. It takes some effort, that much is clear from the way you are struggling. First you force it into the neck of the bottle as far as you can and then you take a spoon and use the handle to force the cork all the way down the neck and inside. There's the cork, bouncing around inside the bottle. So far, so good.

Hand the bottle around and ask if anyone can get the cork out without smashing the bottle or breaking the cork. They'll shake the bottle upside down in the feeble hope that the cork will somehow drop out. But it won't. It's there for keeps, or at least that's how it looks.

"I bet you that I can get that cork out. And I won't damage the cork or the bottle. A ten-spot says I can do it." It seems impossible but it isn't. It isn't free either. If they want to know how it's done, they are going to have to cough up the compulsory ten bucks. But it's worth it — the applause you'll get for accomplishing this stunt is almost as satisfying as the cash you are about to win. Almost.

THE CATCH

This is one of those rare bets in which you really can make good on your promise. No tricks, no fancy phrases, no underhand maneuvers. To make it work you need a thin cloth napkin or, better still, silk scarf. So the time to work the bet is when one of your dinner companions is wearing the appropriate fashion accessory.

You borrow the scarf and work a corner of it into the bottle. Push more and more of the scarf inside until only a handful remains outside. Now shake the bottle around until you can maneouvre the cork onto the scarf.

What you do next is something you just won't think possible until you give it a try.

Pull on the scarf, entangling the cork and drawing it nearer to the neck of the bottle. The narrow end of the cork should be in direct line with the opening in the bottle; you'll probably need to jiggle everything around for a while to get into this position. Now give the scarf one almighty tug. At first the cork will jam in the neck of the bottle, but another long hard pull will free it. Make sure nobody is standing to the side of you, sometimes the cork flies out like...well, like a cork from a bottle!

40 HOLEY SMOKE

THE HOOK

I love this. It's a game the sucker cannot win and it has a spectacular finale. You introduce it by saying it's an old army game that your grandpa showed you. You take a square of paper torn from a napkin, place it over the mouth of a glass and fasten it in place with a rubber band. And on top of the tissue you place a coin.

The game is simple. Each of you takes turns using a lit cigarette to burn a hole in the paper. As more and more holes are burned into the paper, the coin becomes in danger of falling into the glass. Whoever makes the coin drop is the loser. It's like a low-tech version of Kerplunk.

It's actually a really good game and requires a bit of skill and concentration. Not that any of it will help the sucker when you offer to bet the cost of the meal on the next game of *Holey Smoke*.

THE CATCH

This is the only bet in the book that you will need to get a special something for. It's a special kind of paper called "flash paper" and you can buy it in magic and novelty stores. The paper has a special property; it flares up with a bright flash as soon as you touch it with a lit cigarette and vanishes instantly, almost without trace.

By now you should be ahead of me. After a couple of kosher games using ordinary napkin paper, you make the bet and place your sheet of flash paper across the top of the glass, holding it in place with the rubber band. All you have to do is let the sucker take the first turn. As soon as he touches it with his cigarette, the paper disappears in a flash and the coin drops straight into the glass. Play this in front of a big crowd and not only will you get the ten-spot, but a huge belly laugh as well.

THREE

SPORTING CHANCE

"DEPEND ON THE RABBIT'S FOOT
IF YOU WILL—BUT REMEMBER IT
DIDN'T WORK FOR THE RABBIT."
— R.E. SHAW

JIGGERY POKERY

THE HOOK

Who wouldn't like to deal like a demon when it comes to playing cards? A real sharp takes years to develop his craft. Fortunately for you there's a quicker way to your opponent's wallet if you follow this crash course in cardsmanship. How about beating your victim's money out of him even after you've let him pick out his own hand? The proposition goes like this:

You bet the sucker that you can beat him in a game of poker even if you both choose your hands out of a face-up deck. What's more, you'll let him see which cards you pick so that he has a chance to change his hand for a better one. He won't believe you so you spell it out.

"I'll pick five cards – face up. And then you pick five cards. After that we can both discard and draw more cards to make a better hand, just like ordinary poker. Only one rule: all royal flushes are equal. In other words no suit is better than another. Other than that, the wager is that I won't lose or draw. I'll win."

The bit about the suits being equal appears to mean that he could equal your hand no matter what you picked. If you have a royal flush, he can also pick a royal flush. Couldn't be clearer. Could it?

THE CATCH

Here's the swindle. Spread the cards across the table and let him get a good look at them. Encourage him to think about his strategy before choosing. And remind him that he's to pick out five cards to make up a poker hand, but, as you said before, you'll choose first so that he can evaluate your cards.

You open the game by picking out the four tens and any other card. Make it a two or something low. It'll confuse the hell out of him.

Now it's the sucker's turn to choose. If he hasn't already spotted it, he will now realize that whatever winning strategy he had contemplated lies in ruins. Since you have all the tens, he can't draw himself the coveted royal flush. Best hand he can make is four aces. Let him take any five cards he likes.

Remind him you said you'd both draw cards again to see if you could better your hands. This time you discard three of the tens and the odd card, leaving you just one ten. Draw whatever cards are necessary to make the highest straight flush possible. If he holds all the aces, you'll probably end up making a king-high straight flush.

This strategy, drawing to make the highest straight flush, will work no matter which cards he holds. And because the tens you had are now in the discard pile and can't be touched by the sucker, he can never equal it. This makes you a winner and you didn't even have to deal from the bottom of the deck.

42 POKER IN THE EYE

THE HOOK

Maybe letting him select his own cards from the deck in *Jiggery Pokery* was just too much for your meal ticket. Too much choice confused his already overstrained brain. So, to make things simple, you take out just ten cards from the deck.

"I've got ten cards. I'm going to show them to you one at a time and let you pick five. Whichever five are left, those are the ones I'll have for my hand. Couldn't be fairer – you pick five and I have the leftovers. And yet I'm going to bet that, once again, I'll neither lose nor draw. I'll win."

If it got any simpler you'd be reading him bedtime stories. Who could refuse such a bet? He picks five, leaves you with the rest. Only a foolish man would look a gift horse in the mouth. And yet, if he'd looked closely, he'd probably see you smiling.

THE CATCH

No one ever lost money betting on the greed of others and this devious wager depends on your sucker imagining that he smells a free lunch.

The ten cards you remove from the deck are: three tens, three eights, three twos, and the ace of spades. Apart from the ace, the other cards can be from any suit.

Don't let him see which ten cards you're removing from the deck. Shuffle them up a bit, fan them in front of you, and cut the packet to bring the ace of spades to the third or fourth card from the top. You can do all this as you describe the wager to the victim.

Then drop the packet of ten cards face down onto the table. Once the bet has been accepted, hold up the top card of the packet, show it to him, and ask, "Do you want this card or should I have it?" If he wants it, deal it to him. If he thinks you should have it, deal it to yourself.

Go though the entire packet like this, one card at a time until he has five cards. You take the rest. Here's where greed comes in, because as soon as he sees that ace of spades he'll take it. After all it is the highest card in the packet and he's not going to give it to you. Which is a pity because it's the Jonah card of the group. Whoever has that card will lose. And if he takes it, it means you'll always beat him with a full house or two pairs. Try it and see.

43 POKER IN BOTH EYES

THE HOOK

Unlucky suckers – in other words, anyone who has ever accepted one of your wagers – often demand a rematch. In this case you appear to repeat the bet except the conditions are even fairer than before.

This time you give the sucker the ten cards. He shuffles them up to his heart's content and then drops them back on top of the deck. He deals them out, one to you, one to him, until you have five cards each. Well, this time he only has himself to blame. He shuffled. He dealt. He lost.

THE CATCH

When you take the deck, note which card is on top. Let's say it's a four. Now take out any other nine cards made up of three banks of three but not including any fours. For instance, three tens, three twos, three Jacks. Doesn't matter what they are as long as none of them are the same value as the top card. And don't let your mark see their faces.

As you do this, casually say, "I'm going to take out ten cards and we'll use them to play poker." This is a lie. There are only nine cards but no one will question the statement, especially if they've seen you work the *Jiggery Pokery* stunt.

Give the packet of cards to the sucker and ask him to shuffle them. When he's finished, ask him to drop the packet face down on top of the deck you are holding. Then place the deck on the table. Here's the bet:

"You've shuffled and now you're going to deal. One to me, one to you. Yet I'm prepared to bet a ten-spot that I win."

He will be at a loss to see how. But if he deals to you first, as convention dictates, it means that he'll get the four that was originally on top of the deck. This Jonah card will make him the loser and you the winner. Serves him right. He should know better by now.

There's one final twist on this bizarre poker game. If you mark the back of the Jonah card so that you can spot it, you can ask him to pick the ten cards up and give them another shuffle. When he's finished shuffling ask him to deal the cards out into two hands. As he deals, note which hand the marked cards falls to. Now ask him to pick a hand. If he picks the one with the marked card, bet him that you'll win. However, if he picks the other hand, bet him that this time he'll win. If the card falls early you can make this bet before he's even finished dealing. Of course, if he takes it, he might win the game but he's sure to lose his money.

44 FIVE CARD TRICK

THE HOOK

Call it Three-Card Monte, Find the Lady, Sidewalk Shuffle, or a right rip-off, the urge to bet money on your ability to follow a card as it is shuffled around with a few others is irresistible. So much so that one famous gambler, Canada Bill Jones, once offered the Union Pacific Railroad $10,000 if they would let him work the old Three-Card Monte on their trains. He promised that he would only defraud salesmen and Methodist preachers. Oddly enough, they didn't let him.

You have no compunction about playing this version of monte on anyone who happens to come your way bearing a crisp ten-spot. Instead of three cards you use five, which your sucker will at first think is lessening his chances of winning. And that would be the case if it weren't for the following offer:

"All I ask is that you follow the Queen. And to make it as simple as possible, I won't even shuffle them around. I'll just hold them, spread out like this. I'll show you the cards clearly so you can make sure you know where the Queen is. And then I'll turn them facedown. All you have to do is slide this paper clip onto the Queen. Snag the Queen and you're a winner. Snag anything else, and your money's mine."

You hold the cards spread out to show what you mean. The Queen is the middle card of the five. Doesn't look like there is anything funny going on. And as soon as the sucker has taken out his ten-spot, you kindly hand him a paper clip in exchange. "Go on, just put it on the Queen," you say, adding quietly, "Make my day."

You don't use any sleight of hand. And as promised you don't shuffle any cards around. In fact he's certain that he's snagged the Queen. But when the cards are turned faceup, your buddy is stunned to find that he has made a grievous mistake – he accepted your bet.

THE CATCH

It's not the quickness of the hand deceiving the eye this time, but the eye is deceived all the same. The scam depends on a kind of optical illusion.

Take five playing cards, one of which is a Queen. Put the Queen in the

middle and spread the five cards facedown as shown.

Put a paper clip on the card you think is the Queen, i.e., the middle card.

Now turn the fan of cards over. You should be surprised to see that the clip is actually on the right-hand card of the fan. You seem to have missed the Queen completely.

And that's what your sucker discovers when he gives it a try – somehow he's totally missed his appointment with Her Majesty. Pull the right-hand card of the fan out and the paper clip with it and toss it to the table. Collect the ten-spot and pocket it while he grabs the cards to try it again for himself. It's rare that anyone gives the cards back – they're too busy trying their luck on the next easy target that passes by.

THE HOOK

Time to visit the pool table while your buddies are complaining about your card-cheating skills. But don't worry, you don't need to know blue chalk from blue cheese to make the following cool piece of showmanship work. It seems so impossible that people are not only happy to pay up, but they'll even pay you to show them how you cheated.

Walking up to a suitable individual (anyone in possession of a ten-spot) you say, "Ever tried this? A guy showed it to me and I thought it was impossible." Borrow a cigarette – once again you've left yours in the machine – and stand it on its filter end in the center of the table, unlit.

Then arrange three balls close around it, the cigarette standing right in the middle of them.

"Here's the challenge – you've got to hit the cue ball at those three balls, knocking them away but leaving the cigarette still standing."

Let your friend try. He'll find it is absolutely impossible to shoot the cue ball at the others without knocking over the cigarette. He can try all night if he wants to, but he'll never do it.

Then say, "I bet you a five-spot I can do it." Now, he really wants to see this. He's been shooting balls all over the place and he just can't see how that cigarette can be left standing. He'll beg and whimper but you must be strong. Don't do this trick until his five bucks are in your mitt. It's just too good to give away for free.

THE CATCH

The laws of physics provide the solution for this little bit of hustling. When you arrange the balls for your friend to shoot at, you always make sure that the nearest ball is just touching the cigarette. And you always make sure that the two rear balls have a very slight gap between them. Doesn't matter how fast or slow he shoots, that cigarette will hit the deck.

When you arrange the balls for your turn, though, you should pack them tightly so each one is touching the other two but the cigarette is not touching any of them — that's absolutely essential.

Shoot at the ball nearest to you so that you hit it just off-center. Because the balls are packed tightly together they bounce off each other and cannot move inwards to disturb the cigarette. They fly apart leaving the cigarette still standing. It's an amazing thing to watch. So remarkable that your buddy will be begging you for the secret of how you managed it. But secrets don't come cheap. It'll cost him another fiver to learn – after all, it cost you fifty bucks to learn...didn't it?

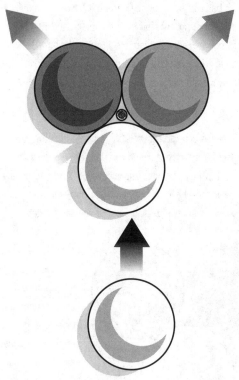

46 BLACK BALLED

THE HOOK

You're playing pool and, to be frank, you're not doing it very well. For once, the guy doing the hustling is not you. You'd taken him on thinking that he was a rank amateur but it turns out that he's a real pro. Finally his lucky streak runs out and it's your turn to shoot. The one thing you know is that if he gets a second chance you're finished. So you give the table a long cool once-over, as if studying all the angles, all the possibilities. You angle your cue this way and that, close one eye as you line up a shot, then move over to the other side of the table to spy out another.

Finally, you announce, "I think I've got you. If I'm right, you're not going to make another shot." He'll laugh in your face. And you in turn will laugh in his. You throw a ten-spot on the table with disdain.

"Ten says you won't make another shot." And now you look damned serious about it. And if he's half the player you think he is (hindsight's a wonderful thing) you know he's sure to take you up on your bet. He's got you beat, at least that's what he thinks, so why not take your ten-spot as well as his anticipated victory?

What he doesn't realize, though, is that although he may be a good player, you're a much better cheat.

THE CATCH

How can you beat a man who's already got you beat? You can't, so you'd better get used to the idea that you won't win this game. But you will win the bet.

And the reason is that you are going to commit a foul by deliberately sinking the 8-ball. And that means the game is over. As I said, you'll lose the game but win the bet, and that's where the money is.

Better be sure you can easily make the shot before making the bet, though. And be sure, too, that you're playing by the rules that mean a foul of this kind means the end of the game and not just a couple of free shots to him.

And don't be too ashamed of taking his money because he'd certainly have been more than happy to take yours. Swindles work best when the sucker is absolutely certain that the odds are in his favor. And when a professional loses out to a rank amatuer, usually they'd much rather hand over the money quietly than make a scene about it.

BERMUDA TRIANGLE

THE HOOK

The Bermuda Triangle: a strange place where the sucker's money mysteriously disappears, never to be seen again.

Taking the triangular frame used to rack up the balls, you balance it upright on the table and then stand a shot of whiskey inside it. You challenge anyone to pick it up and turn it upside down without spilling the drink.

It sounds mad. Dangerous even. But mad and dangerous probably cover most of your buddies and you don't want some idiot swinging the frame around his head in a desperate attempt to meet the challenge. So you quickly add another condition. "Not only will I pick up the frame and turn it upside down and not spill a drop, but I'll do it half a dozen times in less than a minute."

And, just in case they thought there might be some cheating involved (as if), you tell them that you won't touch the glass or its contents. Anyone is welcome to make an attempt before you do but it'll cost them a ten-spot if they spill the whiskey. And all breakages must be paid for. It'll also cost them a ten-spot if they want to see you do it.

THE CATCH

Centrifugal force is the answer, but it's not enough to pick up the rack and start swinging it around like a Russian hammer thrower. First you need to pick it up the right way, and to do that you use the pool cue.

Stick the cue through the top of the frame until it sticks out the other side about a foot.

Now comes the dangerous part. Pick up the cue with both hands just shy of halfway from the fat end, and raise the frame off the table. Now, gently swing the rack side to side on the cue. When you've picked up enough momentum, give the cue an extra swing and you'll be surprised to find that the frame will spin all the way around, upsidedown and back again. And the whiskey will stay in the glass.

On a good day, with the wind in the right direction, you can keep the frame spinning and the whiskey intact for a good half-dozen revolutions. Be careful as you bring it to a halt, though – that's the trickiest part.

If you're feeling really brave, try it with a pint of beer.

 HOT SPOT

THE HOOK

You've just taken the sucker for a Hamilton and he's feeling justly pissed. What he needs is a little spiritual uplift, so you adopt your best evangelist tone and lay a double helping of happiness on it. "Look, I'm a generous guy. Yes indeed my friend, I'm feeling mighty generous of spirit tonight and feel that you of all people deserve a second chance."

Buy him a drink if it makes him feel better because a miserable man makes a poor loser. The joyful are more likely to put their capital at risk. Why, he's smiling already.

You put a ball on the spot and a coin on top of that. "Okay brother, here's the deal. Hit this ball with the cue ball and drop the coin right on the spot. Couldn't be simpler." Or so it seems. He's just got to win this bet, right? Alas, no.

THE CATCH

He'd stand a chance if he set the coin on top of the ball himself, but that's not a chance you're willing to give. When you place the coin on top of the ball, you don't place it dead center. In fact it's deliberately placed at a slight angle. No matter how hard or slow the sucker tries to hit the ball, the coin won't fall down and land on the spot. When *you* try it, you set the coin properly, square on top of the ball.

Give it a good hard smack with the cue ball and the coin will drop straight down to land right on top of the spot.

Amen and hallelujah!

49 YOU'VE BEEN FRAMED

THE HOOK

Arrange three balls in a row, close to the side pocket. Place another ball (X) a short distance from them and challenge the sucker to pocket all three balls with one shot without ever touching the X ball. Just as he's thinking about it, you lay down some conditions. No shots off the cushion, the cue ball can't leave the table and nothing must touch the X ball. Hmm...

THE CATCH

The clue to this caper is in the title because you use the frame to accomplish this little piece of hocus pocus.

Set the frame around the X ball so that its top corner is almost touching the nearest of the three balls.

All you need to do to win the bet is hit the cue ball hard. It will strike the frame and, in turn, the corner of the frame will hit the other balls, knocking them right into the pocket.

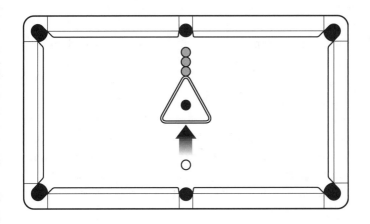

50 PRIVATE DICK

THE HOOK

Not everyone in the world will end up liking you, especially if you keep beating them at every game. Your scheming ways are building up a boil of resentment. Good, because in this scam you take advantage of the fact that your sucker will risk any amount of money to see you fall on your ass.

It begins as a trick of the pick-a-card variety in which you offer to find the sucker's secretly selected card. But something goes wrong; at least that's what the sucker thinks. And he's so sure that you can't find his card that he's prepared to put money on it. But before he can say "abracadabra," once again you've made his money disappear.

THE CATCH

Don't worry if you've never done any magic before and you've got fingers like sausages. This card trick is really easy. It's the way you sell it that makes it an effective swindle.

Take a deck of cards, give it a shuffle, and when you've finished, secretly note the bottom card. This is your "key card." Remember it.

Place the deck face down on the table and say, "Let me show you a trick."

Ask the sucker to cut the deck into two halves and then take the card he cut to, in other words the top card of the former lower half of the deck. That's his selected card. Tell him to remember it, and if he looks like he might be a bit of a doofus, get him to show it to anyone else who is standing around. You can't be too careful. Many a good trick has been ruined by someone saying, "I think it was the three . . . or was it the four . . . of those funny little clover things?"

When he has memorized it, ask him to put it back, but instead of putting it back where he got it from, you make him put it on top of the other half. Just say, "Replace the card," and casually point to the top of the packet. This is critical to the success of the trick, so don't get it wrong otherwise you're going to end up as the doofus.

Ask him to pick up the other (bottom) half of the deck and drop it on top of the other. In effect, what you've done is secretly place your key card above his selected card. Tell him to cut the deck again and complete the cut. He can do this several times. In fact, no matter how many times he does it, your key card will always stay right next to his selected one. By the time he's done cutting, the sucker should be convinced that his card is lost in the deck, and if he doesn't know where it is, how could you?

Looks like a pretty good trick so far. Pick up the deck, saying, "What a lot of people don't realize is that when they take a card they leave fingerprints on it. It's true. I can find your card just by examining your fingerprints."

Ask the sucker to hold out his thumb. Take a good look at it in a Sherlock Holmes style, then nod knowingly and murmur, "Shouldn't be too difficult."

Look carefully at the back of the top card of the deck, then, apparently satisfied that this isn't the card you are looking for, turn it over and deal it face up onto the table. The sucker will think you are looking for fingerprints. You're not. You're looking for your key-card because the next card after it will be his.

Keep turning over cards and dealing them into a pile on the table. Make the pile a messy one so that all the cards can be seen at once.

Every now and then you take another look at the sucker's thumb, then compare it to the back of the top card. At some point during your Sherlock charade your key card will show up. Don't bat an eyelid when it does. Deal it onto the table just like the others. The next card in the pack will be the sucker's card. Remember it and deal it onto the table too, but don't stop; continue examining the backs of the following cards, turning them over and putting them on the table.

Your sucker will be confused by this. He knows you've gone right past his selected card. And if you keep talking up your detective skills ("I've never been wrong…") he'll start to feel a bit smug.

Let a half-dozen or so cards go by and then look at the back of the next card with satisfaction as though you've found something. Then look at his thumb. Then back at the card. "The next card I turn over will be yours," you say. He'll assume you mean the card on top of the deck and since he can see his card already on the table, he won't believe you. Reel him in, saying, "Do you think that's possible?" Whatever he says, turn his response into a wager. "Ten bucks says it is. Ten dollars says the next card I turn over will be yours."

He will be absolutely sure you've got it wrong and his ten-spot shouldn't be long in making an entrance. Put yours on the table beside it. Then say "Okay, ten dollars that the next card I turn over will be yours." Pause, so the full consequence of what you have said sinks in. Then reach over to the pile of cards on the table, pull out his card and turn it face down!

Elementary, my dear Watson.

🔳 CASE DISMISSED

THE HOOK

As far as Mr. Unlucky is concerned, the one redeeming feature of being taken by the *Private Dick* trick is that he might be able to use it on someone else. He's therefore grateful that you've taught him exactly how to do it.

He's thankful too that you've made him practice the trick on you. You wouldn't want him trying it out on some poor mug without getting the details just right, would you?

Okay, all he needs to do now is find himself a sucker. But look; who's this walking into the bar? It's one of your shady pals. "He's a bit of an idiot," you say. "Shouldn't have much trouble with him. Chance to get your money back. Maybe even a bit more. Off you go, man, get it while you can."

And as he ambles away to hook his first victim, you get your drink order in because, once again, you won't be paying for it.

THE CATCH

The sucker has, of course, been set up. While he thinks he's onto a winner, the reality is that he's about to double what he's already lost. The scam goes like this:

He follows all your instructions and reaches the stage where he knows the identity of your friend's card. He can see it right there on the table. The trouble is, your pal knows this trick too. And he knows you've sent this poor jerk over to have his wallet ransacked. So when the would-be Sherlock says "I bet you ten bucks that the next card I turn over will be yours," your buddy answers "Nah, that's impossible!"

Sherlock will tell him that ten bucks says it's not. To which your pal says "Ten bucks? It's worth twenty! Twenty bucks says that the next card you turn over won't be mine."

Talk about pennies from heaven. Sherlock is secretly congratulating himself on making more money from this trick than you did.

"Are we on?" asks your pal. He extends a hand to Sherlock. And as Sherlock is shaking it, he uses his other hand to turn over the cards on the table and mix them around. With them all now face down, Sherlock has just lost his first case.

52 CUT THROAT

THE HOOK

"This is a gentleman's game," you say as you shuffle a deck of cards. "You cut, I cut, and whoever gets the highest card wins."

You ask him to start by cutting off some cards. He does, and cuts to an eight. Now it's your turn. You cut deep, look at the card, and say "Nine, I win!" and then replace the cards on the deck.

Which would be great if you really did cut a nine but your sucker isn't too sure. You didn't actually show him the card you cut to.

"Didn't I explain? This is a gentleman's game. We both trust each other. Don't we?" Truth is he doesn't trust you one bit and he watches carefully as you shuffle the deck again and place it on the table.

"Once more" you say, indicating that he should cut the cards again. This time he cuts a Jack. You make your cut and declare a Queen, but again you quickly replace your cards before he gets a chance to see what you actually did cut to.

"Don't you believe me? Look!" You pick up the deck and spread through it, finding a Queen. "That's the one." Then smile inanely.

"Let's try again. This time, I'll cut first." You do and declare a King. Not surprisingly when the sucker makes his cut he's finally caught onto the game. "I've got an ace" he says, replacing the cards. He beat you, or so it seems. In fact, as the sucker will soon find out, you've just beat him.

THE CATCH

As soon as the sucker claims he cut to an ace, you bet him that he didn't. And he'll probably take it too, expecting that he can do exactly what you did and just pick up the deck, spread through the cards and say, "That's the ace I cut to."

Except, as you might have already guessed, he can't. There are no aces in that deck. You put them in your pocket before you began. Fancy, him trying to cheat you of all people!

53 COLOR BLIND

THE HOOK

"Name a color – red or black?" you say to the sucker. He chooses red and you offer to play him a game of *Color Blind*. He's never heard of it, so, always ready to share your knowledge, you offer to teach him.

"It's simple. You shuffle the deck and then put it down on the table. Then you turn cards over two at a time. If they are both red, you get them. If they are both black, I get them. If one is red and the other is black, nobody gets them. Clear?"

Crystal, and so is the bet: "Whoever ends up with the most cards wins the game. To make sure it's fair, you get to shuffle the cards." The sucker shuffles. He deals. You win.

THE CATCH

I'm not sure exactly how this bet works, only that it does, provided you are using a full deck of fifty-two cards. Before you start playing, you sneak two red cards out of the deck. If the cards are dealt as described, there will always be more black pairs than red pairs.

It's only when the sucker chooses the color that you tell him exactly what the bet is. If he chooses red, say, "Whoever has the most cards wins." If he chooses black, say, "Whoever has the least cards wins." Either way it will be you.

CHASE THE ACE

THE HOOK

You show three cards – an ace, two, and three of clubs – and hand them to the sucker as you invite him to play *Chase the Ace*. "It's the same as Find the Lady," you say, "except you get to mix the cards and I do the betting."

He shuffles the three cards up so that no one knows which is which. Then you ask him to deal one card to himself, one to you, and the third card to himself. He's got two and you've got one.

"Pick up your two cards, look at them. You might have the ace, or you might not. Either way, I want you to deal any card except the ace face up onto the table."

He does, leaving you with one face down card each. "Now, you already have the advantage over me. You've seen two of the cards so you already know whether I've got the ace or whether you have. But I've seen nothing. Is that right?"

He'll agree that it is. "And yet a dollar says I can find the ace. And to prove it, I'll give you ten chances to win."

Sounds fair and yet Lady Luck has already sided with you; it won't be long before his pockets are as empty as a politician's promise.

THE CATCH

You won't win this bet every time. But you will win in the long run, which is why you play for low stakes over ten rounds.

What the sucker doesn't realize is that by dealing himself two of the three cards he's also giving himself two chances out of three of having the ace.

It doesn't matter that he knows where the ace is or that he has turned one of his cards face up. You always bet that the ace is in the hand that originally held two cards. And two out of three times you will be right. Over a long sequence of betting, you will win.

To vary the game have him sometimes deal the two cards to you. Makes no difference; you always bet on the card left over from the hand that once held two cards.

And to confuse him further, every now and then you take three different cards out of the pack and nominate one of them as the card you'll follow.

If you feel that the mathematics of the game really are passing him by, then use four cards and have him deal three into one hand and then turn two of them over. If he'll fall for that, he'll fall for anything.

LIMBO

THE HOOK

Let's face it: you're a lousy pool player. You couldn't sink a ball if there were a dozen pockets on the table. That's why if you want to beat the sharks you're going to have to do it with brains rather than skill. And if you want to try some of the following bets you'd better be fast on your feet as well. Or at least have some big pals standing by.

You pick up a cue, study it carefully, and pretend to weigh it between your hands. Then you lay it across the table, with each end resting on opposite cushions near the side pockets.

With the cue in that position, you challenge the sucker to pick up a ball and roll it under the cue.

It doesn't look impossible. The sucker will think that if he rolls the ball hard enough at the thin end of the cue it might be enough to make it jump up out of the way. It won't. And in any case you tell him, "When the ball's gone under, the cue has to be in the same position that it started." That should give him pause for thought.

THE CATCH

All you asked him to do was roll the ball under the cue. And that's exactly what you do as you roll the ball along the floor...under the table!

You can get caught out on this – always check the table you're working with to make sure that there is a gap below it to roll the ball through; some automated tables don't have one.

56 HEAD SOUTH

THE HOOK

"An eight year old kid could do this one...with twenty years practice," you say. "All you have to do is reverse the triangle like this."

There are ten balls in the frame and they make a neat triangle which points north. You then turn the frame around, complete with balls, until the tip points south.

"That's all you have to do; turn the triangle around so that the balls point in the opposite direction. There are two problems though. The first is that you can't use the frame. The second is that you can only move three of the balls. Move three balls and make the triangle point the opposite way. You've got five minutes. Off you go!"

THE CATCH

This is a real brainstrainer. It's so easy when you use the triangle but doing the same thing by moving only three of the balls is an entirely different story. It can be done and, as usual, the answer is simple when you know how. Fortunately for you, the sucker doesn't.

The illustration explains everything you need to know. The balls at the tips of the triangle are the ones that you need to move. The only thing the sucker will be moving is money from his wallet to yours.

THE MONEY SHOT

THE HOOK

There you are playing the legendary Typhoon Ted, house champion for more years than you care to remember. Ted is as dumb as the brush he's usually pushing along Main Street, but he's a damn good pool player and, as usual, you take a beating at the table. Still, all is not lost and at the end of the game you bluster Typhoon into a little wager.

First you get a ten-spot from him, square it up with one of your own, and fasten them together with a paper clip you just happen to have handy. The clipped notes are placed on the table and then a ball set on top of them both. You place the 8-ball just in front of a side pocket and the cue ball on the opposite side of the table.

"The challenge is to start with a ball on top of the bills. Then you have to pocket the 8-ball in the side pocket without hitting that ball. Also, you can't hit a cushion and the cue ball can't leave the table. Winner takes all."

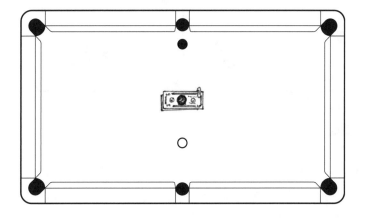

Even Typhoon Ted will think this is impossible unless he's a wizard at making curve shots. But his cash is already on the table and he won't be getting it back unless he figures out how to make that shot.

THE CATCH

When Typhoon Ted has tried and failed, you repeat the conditions of the challenge. "The ball starts on top of the bills." As you say this you pick the ten-spots up and roll them into a tube. Use the paperclip to keep the tube closed. Then balance the ball on top of the rolled-up bills.

"You can't hit that ball but I didn't say anything about hitting the notes."

You now shoot the cue ball at the rolled-up bills. It knocks the tube out of the way and, if you've hit it right, carries on and pockets the 8-ball.

"No cushions or jump shots either. I think you'll agree that fulfills the terms of the bet." Best buy Typhoon a drink after this one. Looks like he's had the wind knocked right out of him.

58 CUELESS

THE HOOK

You've done just about everything but actually play a game of pool to achieve your near legendary reputation. Once again you're about to display your prowess when it comes to ball control. And this time you're not even going to use a cue; just one finger will do the trick!

You place a ball up on the cushion at one end of the table with your index finger holding it in place. Your sucker does the same with another ball. The challenge is to press down on the ball and squirt it up the table as far as you can. Your bet is that you can squirt your ball further than they can.

Now the great thing about this challenge is that everyone can play along – so long as they have a ten-spot that is. And the more the merrier, for you will indeed beat all takers. But let them all take their turn first and mark their distances on the table with chalk. Then, show them how an expert does it.

THE CATCH

This simple challenge is trickier than it looks. Anyone pushing down hard on the ball in the hope that mere pressure will cause it to travel further up the table will be in for a shock. Pressing down causes backspin and so the ball not only won't squirt very far but after a short while will start rolling backwards.

Not so when you press down on your ball, however, because you've secretly wet the tip of your finger (with saliva or just dip it in your drink when no one is looking). This lessens the friction between the ball and your fingertip and prevents backspin; you'll have no trouble getting the ball all the way up the table. From then on, it's a short step to a night of free drinks.

59 BOX CLEVER

THE HOOK

You play a little game of monte with the sucker. He hides a ten-dollar bill in one of three packs of cigarettes while your back is turned. The bet is this: if you find the box containing the ten-spot, you keep it. If you fail, you pay him double the stake. Looks like a winner for him but the truth is you cannot fail.

THE CATCH

You need three packs of cigarettes for this trick. At first glance they all look alike, but in fact one of them is marked so you can distinguish it from the other two. It can be any kind of a secret mark; a nick, a dot, a slightly dented corner. Anything that you will notice but the sucker won't.

Now pay attention – there's money resting on this. Set the three cigarette boxes out in front of the sucker with the marked one to your left.

You can see the mark from where you are.

Tell him that when your back is turned he should place his ten-spot inside one of the boxes then put it back in position.

Okay, let's assume he's done that. Now tell him to swap the positions of the other two boxes. And when he's satisfied, he should just make sure that all the boxes are once again in a straight line.

Believe it or not, as soon as you turn around you will be able to tell him which box contains the money. It's easy. Just look for the box you marked. If the box is still at the left end of the row, then that's the box with the money.

If the marked box is at the right end of the row, then the money is in the middle box. And if the marked box is in the middle of the row, then the money is in the box on the right.

Nothing more to it. You will win his money every time. And with a little bit of practice you'll be able to calculate which box the money is in no matter where the marked box starts. It's just a matter of applying a little logic and common sense. It also makes an ideal follow up to *Matchbox Monte*. Take the matches out and use the sucker's money instead.

A word of warning, though: never turn your back on a player unless you have a friend nearby to keep an eye on him. You don't want him mixing the boxes up any old way the moment your eyes are off him. That wouldn't be fair play, would it?

⑥⓪ DICING WITH DEBT

THE HOOK

Dice are the ultimate symbols of fate. The very tools of Lady Luck herself, used since time immoral in games of chance the world over. If you could control the dice, you could control the future. Okay, maybe that's a little overstated, but you could certainly win a few bucks from your gullible pals. So, after a skillful game like backgammon, in which you exhibited no skill whatsoever, you redeem yourself with this little stunt.

"What do you think the chances are of us rolling the same numbers on the dice?" you ask. The sucker tries his best to calculate the odds but frankly he doesn't have a clue how, so he'll probably come up with some nonsense like "million to one." Fine. You're not teaching a class on probability. As long as he realizes it's difficult, that's all that matters.

"Well, I bet that if you throw these two dice, I might not be able to throw the exact same numbers as you – that would be almost impossible – but I bet I can throw the same total. So if you throw ten, I'll throw ten."

Let this sink in. It's actually highly unlikely that you'd be able to do this but it lays the foundation for the next line you're going to bait him with.

"I'm so confident that I reckon I can let you throw the dice, add up the top numbers and the bottom numbers, and then I'll take the same two dice and throw exactly the same total. How does that sound?"

It sounds very impressive. Surely it's twice as difficult as your first proposition? You'll match whatever total he throws. And that includes not just the top numbers but the bottom ones as well. What are the odds on that?

THE CATCH

The odds are 100 percent in your favor!

All good dice, and this includes ones found in kid's board games as well as casinos, are made in a particular way. The top and bottom numbers of every die (yes, that *is* the singular!) always add up to seven. Not a lot of people know that, not even Michael Caine. And if your sucker happens to be one of the people who does, then he won't accept the bet in the first place and all you've cost yourself is mild embarrassment.

This design factor means that if the sucker rolls two dice and adds both top and bottom numbers, he will always arrive at a total of fourteen. And if you roll two dice, although you will probably not end up with the same numbers showing on top, they will also total fourteen. It's a sure thing.

You disguise this oddity of the dice by first having him roll the two dice and add up the top numbers. Then have him turn one dice over and add the bottom number. Then he turns the second dice over and adds the bottom number on that one. That way he reaches the total of fourteen without ever noticing that each dice added up to seven. Go through the same procedure when totalling the numbers on your dice.

Oh, and don't try it twice on the same sucker. That really would be pushing your luck.

FOUR

MASTERMIND

"BEHIND EVERY GREAT FORTUNE
THERE IS A GREAT CRIME."
— HONORE DE BALZAC

61 WEAKEST LINK

THE HOOK

Whatever happened to the good old American dive? That comfy place that was just like home – dirty and full of crazies. A place where you could get a quiet beer, a game of darts, and be sure to hear some old guy going on about football.

Okay it was boring, but at least there weren't any bar quizzes. When you got caught drinking under age by your history teacher he didn't ask you to name five dead British prime ministers for ten points.

Trouble is there's a new breed of "experts" who, instead of spending their time working on genetic engineering at Princeton, are sitting at McSorley's shouting, "Easy!" Time for revenge.

Within earshot of your local "expert," your pal, whom you've primed in advance, holds up a bit of paper and says, "No way, not in sixty seconds you can't."

"Maybe I can't, but I bet Keith can. He's been bar quiz champ two years running, right, Keith?" you say.

"Three," corrects Keith, and with praise as bait, wanders over to the killing field.

"Keith could do it easily, couldn't you, Keith – answer one lousy quiz question in sixty seconds?"

Now Keith is not going to wager any money on this stunt – not right away anyhow. So you wring the cash out of him by appealing to his ego. "I'll bet a ten-spot he can. You can do it, can't you, Keith?"

He'll hem and haw but the main thing he'll want to know is where the question came from. "My kid's school" is always a good answer. "That Millionaire quiz" is another. But "the bar quiz down the road" is sure to hook him.

So put your ten-spot on the table then look at Keith and ask him for his.

I mean, if you've got such confidence in him, shouldn't he have confidence in himself? You might need a crowbar to get his wallet open but the one thing more precious to a trivia addict than his cash is his pride.

THE CATCH

Take the question paper off your stooge and place it face down in front of Keith. Have someone time him, turn the paper over, and off you go. Here's the question:

Marie's father has five daughters:

1 - Chacha

2 - Cheche

3 - Chichi

4 - Chocho

5 - ? ? ? ? ? ?

What is the fifth daughter's name?

Keith, if he's bright, will stare at it for maybe thirty seconds, work out the vowel sequence, and come up with the name of "Chuchu" – easy. But he's wrong. The name of the fifth daughter is "Marie." Didn't his teacher tell him to read the question carefully?

One thing's for sure. He won't forget your name in a hurry. Be nice though – at least give him the dignity of waiting until he's gone before you and your pal buy the next round using his cash.

62 CASH IN HAND

THE HOOK

You hold up your closed fist and say, "I've got three coins in my hand, and they add up to sixteen cents." This is an unmistakable challenge to Einstein, Keith's best and equally brainy pal.

"So?" says Einstein.

"So, one of them isn't a dime," you reply. He's been playing that quiz machine all evening like a man possessed and making a killing so it's time you relieved him of some of his loose change. He thinks about it for a while. Sixteen cents, three coins, and yet one of them isn't a dime. You can see his forehead furrowing. Finally he decides that such a thing can't be right.

"Oh yes it can," you say. "And I'll bet a ten-spot that I'm telling the truth: three coins, they add up to sixteen cents, and yet one of them isn't a dime."

"You're bluffing."

"Am I?"

When you see the sweat starting to collect in those furrows you know you've got him.

"Let's see the color of your money," you say, taking a bill from your pocket. It's unfair really. He's an information junkie. He wants to know. He must know, even if he has to pay ten bucks for the answer. You rustle the crisp ten-spot between your fingers. He still thinks you're bluffing, but he doesn't know for sure. The only thing for certain is that it's going to cost him to find out. Soon he will be stacking the stream of silver that tumbled from the quiz machine. And ten bucks of it will be yours.

THE CATCH

When you find a man of words, it's nice to beat him up with them, so be careful how you phrase this bet. When you open your hand, you reveal a dime, a nickel, and a penny. That's sixteen cents in total. Ah, you think, but when Einstein sees the coins he is going to say, "You said one of the coins wasn't a dime." So you did, and to prove it you pick up the penny saying, "This one isn't a dime," and then the nickel, "and, now that I come to think of it, actually this one isn't either."

Game, set, and match.

🔞 WORD UP

THE HOOK

Einstein is at the bar sipping his grapefruit juice and his girl Marilyn is by his side with the cheapest drink that money can buy. He's a clever guy but mean as hell. *Jeopardy* is on the television and he's shouting out the answers. Marilyn's not impressed. She's seen it all before. He's just such a smart-ass. But there's smart and then there's street smart.

Sensing your moment, you go up to him and say "Tell me, Einstein, how long do you think it would take to list a hundred words that don't have the letter A in them?" Knowing him it won't be long. So you up the stakes. "Okay, how long to think of a hundred different words that don't have the letters A or B in them?" Again, that's no problem for Einstein but wouldn't it be better if Marilyn could name them? I mean, Einstein doesn't even think she knows a hundred words. Which is great, because here's the bet:

"I bet that me and Marilyn can name a hundred words without the letters A, B, C, J, K, M, P, Q, or Z in them. Can't we Marilyn? And we'll do it in less than five minutes."

Marilyn will now have the look of a deer caught in headlights. "No way, I can't do that," she protests. But you don't listen to her. "In fact, I'll just name five of the words and I bet Marilyn can name the other ninety-five, isn't that right Marilyn?"

Now that's just too good an offer to turn down. Whatever other charms Marilyn may possess, she isn't known for her intellect, and before you can say "Potent Potables" the bait has been taken and the money is as good as yours.

THE CATCH

When called upon to deliver you start to count: "One, two, three, four, five," and then you turn to Marilyn and prompt her to continue the count up to one-hundred, saying, "You can continue from there Marilyn, one hundred words and believe it or not, none of them have the letters A, B, C, J, K, M, P, Q, or Z in them. By the way, what are you drinking? He's paying."

64 OUT FOR THE COUNT

THE HOOK

You walk into the bar and see Einstein, still watching *Jeopardy*. Once again he's getting all the answers right and everyone around the bar is completely pissed off. You get your drink order in, go up to Einstein, pat him on the back, and say, "Nice going. You never seem to get anything wrong, do you? In fact, I don't think you could get a question wrong if you tried." He'll quite rightly look at you with some suspicion, still steamed when he remembers the last bet that you won. So you reassure him that you have no hidden agenda, which of course you do. "No, really, I bet if I asked you some questions, you couldn't give me five wrong answers in a row."

Wrong answers? He's never given a wrong answer in his life so it's best to clarify what you mean. "I mean, I ask you five questions and you give me five deliberately wrong answers. For instance, I ask you your name, you tell me it's Yoda. I ask you what two plus two is, you say five. Got it?"

He's got it but you've still got to reel him in. "In fact, you're so damn brainy that I'm prepared to bet ten bucks that you can't give me five wrong answers." You lay your dough on the table. He thinks about it. "Go on, Einstein," you say, like a man trying to do him a good turn. A man trying to make amends for taking his money along with his dignity. "I know you'll win this one." His ten-spot hits the table, Hamilton blinking in the light, and you proceed to hit him with the questions. Need I say he doesn't get them all wrong?

THE CATCH

Pull this one off and you'll get an Oscar. Here are the questions:

Point to his ten-spot on the table and ask: "What's that?" He can answer with anything he likes as long as he doesn't give the right answer. "Good, that was an easy one." Turn to Marilyn and say, "What's her name?" Hmm. He'll be looking for a bit of trickery there. There isn't any and after due thought he'll give a nonsense answer, probably something Freudian like "Mother."

Point to one of the drinks and ask, "Is this glass full or empty?" He gives an answer. Pause for thought and then ask, in a very casual way, "How many questions is that?" Say it as if you've lost count. Now he may smell a rat at this point and if he does, it's you, because this is a trick question. It is possible he'll give you the right answer, three, in which case he loses the bet. But a smart guy like Einstein will probably see through it, and he'll give you some other answer. This is where your acting skills come in.

"You clever SOB!" Give a laugh and pretend to have been caught at your own game. Einstein has beaten you. Let him think he's won. "You did well, pal, you deserve a drink for that. Marilyn, get him a drink, the boy done good." And then very casually ask, "Have you heard that one before?" And lulled by your manner he will say no. And that's when he loses the bet, because you said you'd ask him five questions, and this is the fifth. He'll need that drink.

65 WHAT'S THE SCORE?

THE HOOK

Today's the day of the Super Bowl and Fred the Football Freak is by the bar recalling the outcome of the last fifty Bowls and speculating about this one. There's nothing he doesn't know when it comes to football statistics and the guys are asking questions because they're running a pool on who is going to score first. So you wander up and say, "I've got a bet for you. Never mind who scores first, I bet I can tell you what the score will be before the game even starts." He'll reel out some figures and probabilities and talk about who is playing and in what positions, but before he can bore you to tears you interrupt, "No, what I mean, Fred, is that right here and now I can tell you what the score will be before they've even touched the ball. In fact, I've written it down."

You take an envelope out of your pocket and place it on the bar. "And I bet you a ten-spot I'm right. Anyone else want to take that bet?" Look around for any likely suckers as you take out your wallet and lay a ten-spot on the envelope to show that you mean business. Unless you've already cleaned out this neighborhood, you're about to go home a winner.

THE CATCH

You said you knew what the score would be before the game started. So you did. It was 0–0. It always is before the game starts, and that's what you wrote down in the envelope! Make sure the exit's in sight and you're wearing your running shoes when you work this one.

66 PROPHETEERING

THE HOOK

Keith's back. He's still not forgiven you for that five daughters question and Einstein has been telling him what a complete conman you are. So has Marilyn. Well, you didn't think it would last did you? Basically, he's looking for revenge. And to make matters worse it's raining outside and your pockets are as empty as Marilyn's head. So you quickly conjure up another bet.

"Keith, what do you know about wildlife?" you ask. Fact is he knows more than the Crocodile Hunter did, but don't let that stop you. "Well, here's a question for you. It was the rain that inspired me," you say, lying. "And there's a ten-spot for a correct answer. Ready?" Taking his blank look as a yes, you've got yourself a bet. "Okay, tenner to you if you get it, tenner to me if you lose." Without pausing to give him a chance to back out, you say, "Well, it's a biblical question: how many animals did Moses take on the ark with him?"

A bright guy like Keith will usually answer almost immediately. "Two of each." And, of course, he'd be wrong.

THE CATCH

The correct answer is none. Moses didn't take any animals onto the ark. That was Noah!

Of course it's just possible that Keith catches you out on this one. He might be sharper than you imagine. Somewhat cockily he could say, "It wasn't Moses, it was Noah." In which case you play the fool, saying, "Oh, yeah. Stupid me. I could have sworn it was Moses. We'll forget that one. Who was Moses anyway?" Immediately you'll get a long and dull discourse on Moses and, with his irresistible urge to show off his knowledge, Keith will have forgotten entirely about the bet so you won't have to pay out. There will always be another chance to drain the brain of his cash.

TIME OF THE MONTH

THE HOOK

Looking along the bar you see that Keith has a PDA. Either that or he's trying to beam himself up to another planet. For the uninitiated, a PDA is a personal digital assistant. It's an electronic miracle, a handheld computer in which you can keep notes, your schedule, or, as Keith is doing now, quiz questions. Does everything a notepad and pen does except it costs a lot more and if you drop it your entire life disappears. Still, it provides you with a good opening salvo in the perpetual war of wagers.

"I've heard those things are really bad for you."

"What are you talking about?" says Keith, tapping his tiny screen.

"Read it in the paper. They say people depend on them too much. They forget the everyday things of life."

"Like what?" He switches the machine off and puts it away, suddenly looking a little scared that you've set your beady eyes on it and might be about to embark on some devious scheme in an attempt to make it your own. As if.

"For instance," you say, "before computers were invented, you exercised your brain more. If you wanted to remember something you used a poem or a little rhyme or saying. That way it stuck in your mind. I bet your memory's not half as good since you got that thing."

As usual Keith will disagree and so, for the obligatory ten-spot, you offer to put him to the test. "Okay, remember the old poem about the number of days in a month? Well, without looking at the calendar in your computer, how many months have thirty days in them?"

He'll smile. PDAs aren't like cell phones. They don't toast your brain to a crisp. The old rhyme is as clear to him now as it was when he first heard it. Which is great, because as long as he starts working out whether each month has thirty or thirty-one days, you've trapped him in yet another mind field.

THE CATCH

Talking about computers and the old rhyme has led Keith down a blind alley. There's only one answer to the problem and it is unlikely to occur to him. Every month has thirty days in it, except for February!

Think about it. And if it still makes no sense, maybe you should get yourself one of those PDAs.

68 SHAKEN AND STIRRED

THE HOOK

To the mastermind, nothing is more attractive than a puzzle to be solved. Not even the lovely Marilyn. When the likes of Einstein and Keith get together over a puzzle, the rest of the world might as well not exist.

You offer to show them something you saw on television last night. "Absolutely amazing, no one could get it," you say, implying that if either of the brainiacs were able to solve it, they would be worthy of your praise, and the ten-spot you're offering. Should they not manage to get it, then they owe you the same. "They only had a minute to do it on TV," you explain, "but I'll give you five minutes to make it fair. After all, some of the kids on that quiz show are pretty clever." That should wind them up.

The puzzle looks simple as you lay out eight matches to make a simple diagram of two glasses. "Imagine they're two Martini glasses. All we need now is an olive." You take out a coin and invite one of the suckers to place the olive into one of the glasses.

"Here's the puzzle. You can't touch the olive but you've got to get it out of the glass. You can touch the matches though. The only problem is that you can only move two of them. That's it; move two matches, get the olive out of the glass, and still have two glasses at the end. Your five minutes start now!"

And it will be five very slow minutes indeed for the two unfortunate suckers.

THE CATCH

This puzzle has been around for a long time and it's usually done with just one "glass." But using two glasses makes it even stronger, especially if your suckers really are puzzle addicts. The second glass acts as a red herring, making them think of building an extra glass in the space between the existing ones. And it prevents them from discovering the real solution, which is to simply rearrange the matches so that one glass is now upside-down.

It doesn't matter which glass they drop the coin in to start with. Just make sure that the two glasses are more than a matchstick's length apart. You want it to look as if their proximity offers a solution. But you don't want either of these sleuths to actually find one!

69 DIAMONDS ARE FOREVER

THE HOOK

Here's another match puzzle and one that seems to offer some hope of a solution to the brainy ones. In reality it's just another scam.

You start by laying out five matches in a diamond formation.

"The bet is to take away three matches and then add two. And yet be left

with exactly the same design as you see here: the diamond."

With challenges of this kind it's always best to set a time limit and for very good reasons. First, some people will take all day about it and for the sake of pride just refuse to give up even when you've got them beat. And second, you want your money! Five minutes is usually enough time but even if you gave them the entire day they probably wouldn't solve this little stunner.

THE CATCH

Expect to be questioned all the way through this one as the sucker tries to solve the puzzle. But be firm and only repeat the terms of the wager, that they should take away three matches and add two and still be left with exactly the same diamond design as they started with.

Here's how you do it. First press your fingers against the lower triangle of matches and then draw them down towards you, saying, "I've taken away three matches."

Now pick up the upper two matches and add them to the triangle, once again making up the diamond shape as you say, "And I add two matches.

I've taken away three and added two. And the diamond looks exactly the way it did before."

They may kick themselves but they can't complain you didn't do exactly as you promised. Now it's their turn to do exactly as they promised, and hand over their hard-earned greenbacks.

⑩ PYRAMID POWER

THE HOOK

Here's another brain buster to test even the most geometrically adept. You lay three matches on the table, saying, "It's easy to make a triangle out of three matches but how many triangles can you make out of six?"

There will be some discussion about this, to which you will listen carefully as if weighing out the answers. Then, having heard what your potential suckers have to say you make the following wager: "I bet I can make more triangles than you can. Not the same amount, but more." Let that sink in for a while. They've already explored some of the options and they can't see how you can possibly do better than they can unless, of course, you cheat. You quickly reassure them on that point.

"I'll make more triangles than you can. And the conditions are that you can't break any matches, you can't add any more matches, and all the triangles must be the same size. Ten-spot says I can. And remember, I have to beat you to win. Time limit on the contest is five minutes. And I'll take on everyone at the same time. Is that a deal?"

Assuming that their combined heads can beat your one, they accept the challenge. And unless they know something you don't, the most they will be able to make with their matches is two triangles. I've never seen anyone make three. You, however, are about to make four!

THE CATCH

The secret to this stunt is given away in the title. Your four triangles are made up of the sides of a three-dimensional pyramid.

When constructing it, work on a tablecloth rather than a polished bar top. It will take a bit of care to build but it can be done quickly once you've got the knack.

The pyramid might not be as impressive as the ancient Egyptian ones but it does possess a curse — everyone who sees it will lose money!

11 THEORY OF RELATIVITY

THE HOOK

This is one for the puzzle brigade. You know the kind. They say things like, "A plane crashes on the border between Mexico and America. And it's full of Swedish pastry chefs. Where do they bury the survivors?" And if you're a couple of sheets to the wind you spend the next half hour talking about international law. At the end of which the smart-ass who asked the question laughs and says, "Idiot. You don't bury survivors." Ha ha.

Well, this one's for him. Get him talking about his favorite topic: himself and his seemingly endless knowledge of trivia. Then hit him with this one. "Can a man legally marry his widow's sister?" It has all the hallmarks of a trick question and he'll seize the bait immediately, explaining that if the man has a widow then he must be dead. And dead men can't marry.

"That's not true," you say. "I think a man can marry his widow's sister. In fact I'm sure of it." So sure that you're willing to place a small wager on it.

THE CATCH

It is in fact possible. The loophole through which dead men can marry their widow's sister is simple. They marry the sister first!

So a man met two sisters, married one of them and then, realizing what a nut-job she was, got divorced. He then married the other sister. Unfortunately she was even madder than the first and drove him to an early grave. His death wasn't in vain though as it enabled you to say that a dead man did indeed legally marry his widow's sister, thereby inadvertently earning you a ten-spot!

⑫ THE PRICE IS RIGHT

THE HOOK

You can turn almost any trick question into a bet if you set it up in the right way. It's a matter of conjuring up a believable story and making it a challenge that's impossible to resist. So when you say to your buddy Mickey, "No, no don't tell them, let's see if they can guess," Keith and Einstein's ears start to burn.

"Guess what?" says Keith.

"Guess how much Mickey's latest purchase just cost him," you reply. "I'll give you a clue. One costs a dollar but you can get twelve for two bucks. And Mickey's bought a hundred and forty-four. How much do you reckon it cost him?"

Mickey nods. He would; he's been promised half the winnings. "And if you can tell me what Mickey paid, I'll give you ten bucks. But if you can't – and I'll give you a minute to discuss it – you owe me a ten-spot."

And since no one, especially Keith and Einstein, like an unsolved mystery, the bet is almost sure to be on.

THE CATCH

The answer is three bucks! Sounds improbable until you prompt Mickey to pull the merchandise out of his pocket. Keith and Einstein should be feeling pretty stupid as Mickey produces three plastic numbers for his front door. That's right; a dollar each and he just happens to live at a hundred and forty-four!

⓭ DIVIDE AND CONQUER

THE HOOK

Okay, so you knew it was going to happen. Keith and Einstein have taken the bar quiz trophy again and won themselves twenty bucks and a pitcher of beer. So what?

So what?! They've got twenty unexpected bucks on them, that's what. And you've got just enough time to get to them before they reach the bar and squander it all on pork rinds.

"You did well there boys," you say, preparing for the kill. "There's not much you two don't know about is there?" With any luck your goading will encourage a bit of bragging on their part. You follow it up, saying, "But I've got a little problem that just might baffle even you."

People who have just won money often have a carefree attitude to their winnings. That's why most gamblers usually end up broke. And that's why Keith and Einstein will take up your challenge.

You take three empty glasses and ten coins and spread them out on the table. "Here's the problem. That guy Sid who always wins the quiz down the road said he'd give this ten-spot to anyone who could solve it." Place the bill on the table too. The likelihood of anyone entrusting you with his cash under any circumstances is negligible but this fact seems to bypass Einstein and Keith who are still drunk with victory.

"How can you divide the coins up so that they're all used and there's an odd number in each glass? I've got to tell you, it sounded simple when I first heard it, but it took me ten minutes to work it out. Sid bet that you can't solve it any quicker, and here's his ten-spot to prove it. Want to match his bet?"

You mentioned Sid because Keith and Einstein don't have a high opinion of him. They also don't have one of you so the thought that you solved the problem at all, never mind in ten minutes, will put them in fighting mode.

But when their ten minutes are up, they're going to have to hand over a ten-spot if they want to find out the answer, just like you had to hand over your soda pop and chips at school for a loan of their homework. It's been a long while coming but it's payback time.

THE CATCH

The problem can't be solved in any mathematical way. Einstein and Keith are not going to be able to divide ten coins into three glasses and leave an odd number in each. But if you look at the problem from a different angle, with a bit of lateral thinking, you can come up with a solution. Put two coins in one glass, three in another glass and five in the third. That distributes all the coins but doesn't leave an odd number in each glass.

However, you rectify that by stacking the glass which contains five coins inside the one that has two.

If you count up, you'll see that each glass now has an odd number of coins in it. No one said anything about keeping the glasses separate. And strangely enough no one bothered to ask.

NEGATIVE EQUITY

THE HOOK

"I don't know what it is, maybe it's because I banged my head as a kid, but I sometimes get these psychic flashes. Premonitions I think you call them." Marilyn knows all about premonitions. She's been having psychic flashes all her life, especially after a glass of wine or two. So she listens with genuine interest, bless her. Keith, however, is skeptical.

Concerned by his cynicism, you offer a demonstration of your paranormal skills. "I bet I can send a thought into Marilyn's mind. No, not that sort of thought. It will be a word. I'll write a word down, concentrate on it, and I bet Marilyn can guess what it is."

Keith is not sure what kind of stunt you're pulling, but he's pretty sure that you haven't managed to set anything up with Marilyn ahead of time. You write something down on the back of an envelope, look at Marilyn as if concentrating, and say, "Marilyn, in a moment I am going to ask you to think of a simple word. Don't worry, it's easy to spell. But I really need you to concentrate hard if this is going to work."

Then you turn to Keith and say, "I'm pretty sure this will work. How about a little side bet? If Marilyn gets it right, you buy the drinks. If she gets it wrong, the drinks are on me."

Keith won't have the faith in Marilyn that you have, which is a pity because Marilyn is about to have another one of her flashes.

THE CATCH

How can Marilyn possibly guess the word you have written down? By your cunning is the answer.

The word you write down is "NO." Write it in capital letters and make some extra fake movements with your pen so that it is not obvious to anyone that the word only has two letters. Now, to get Marilyn to call out this word you employ a very special method of questioning her.

You say "Now before we do this I have to reassure you that we've not arranged anything beforehand. I've written a word down on this paper. At the moment Marilyn, do you have any idea which word I've written down? Yes or no?"

And she will, in all honestly, answer "No." At which point you immediately turn over the envelope and show that she is correct.

Marilyn might not get the joke but Keith will. He'll also be getting the drinks.

15 GOT YOUR NUMBER

THE HOOK

Having proved Marilyn's talent for mind reading, you kindly give Keith a chance to win his money back. "Just a bit of fun, Keith, but here's where you get your revenge. Remember, though, that this one's for real. And for a ten-spot of course."

You write something on the back on an envelope and place it writing side down on the table. "No words this time. I've written a number. A number between one and a hundred. Now, when I snap my fingers I want you to think of a number. Has to be between one and a hundred, though. Understand?"

You're making a big performance of this. Taking control so that Keith only talks when you want him to. There's no time for joking around if you want to win this bet.

"And I bet I've written down the number you're going to think of. Only one condition. You can't change your mind. It's just like on TV; I can only accept your first answer. Got it?"

Keith's got it all right. "Okay, let's go." You snap your fingers, Keith thinks of a number, and you win your bet. How?

THE CATCH

By more verbal dexterity that's how. When you snap your fingers, you look at Keith and say, "Are you thinking of one?" And if he has been following your cues all along he will automatically respond by saying yes. You jump on that word, saying, "He thought of the number one," and then turn over the envelope on the table to reveal that you wrote down the number one.

Keith will immediately protest but as far as you are concerned his complaints go unheard. You repeat the conditions of the bet, that the first answer he gave is the only one you can accept.

STANDING ON CEREMONY

THE HOOK

In trying times people bond together. Friendship in the face of adversity. Now you might think that, having conned Keith out of his cash in the previous two stunts, he would be your worst enemy. But experience shows that the reverse is true. He's already lost his money. The best thing that can possibly happen to him is to watch someone else lose theirs. So when Einstein comes wandering up to see what's going on, you'll find Keith just standing by while you take his buddy on a visit to the cleaners.

"Listen, Einstein. I was just showing Keith here my remarkable psychic abilities. My mother says it's a gift. It would have to be, I never pay for anything."

A little humor, no matter how bad, can work wonders in these situations. If Keith smiles, he's effectively giving you the go ahead to try a scam on his buddy.

"It's uncanny, really. Like Spiderman; a sort of tingling sensation. Look, I'll show you. Think of a word and write it down on this piece of paper. Don't let me see it."

Einstein scribbles away. It'll probably be something with thirty-plus letters that no one but him and the people that compile the Oxford English Dictionary know how to spell. But don't let that worry you.

"Good, now put the paper on the floor, writing side down, and stand on top of it. We don't want anyone touching it. Laboratory conditions, this is."

"Now, I've just done this for Keith and Marilyn." You lie but it looks similar to what you've been doing so you won't get any argument from them. "And I'm getting everything right. No mistakes. What would you say if I could tell you what's on that paper? Before you speak, let me answer that for you. You'd say it's a miracle. But a miracle is what I'm going to do. My intuition is really rocking today so I'm prepared to bet a ten-spot that I can tell you what it is. Is it a deal?"

If he wavers, appeal to Keith and Marilyn. They might be friends with Einstein but they'd still like to see him taken down.

THE CATCH

What's on that paper? Well, Einstein is, of course. He's standing there like a dork with his feet on it and that's what you tell him. Time now to rely on your two strongest assets – an unnaturally thick skin and a selective deafness when it comes to people asking for refunds.

TOURIST TRAP

THE HOOK

English is a funny language. Has a lot of strange rules that make it difficult for even the natives to spell it properly. All that *i* before *e* except after *c* nonsense. Add to that the current fad for text messaging in which nothing is spelled properly and you have a language under siege. This bothers the likes of Einstein and Keith, who consider themselves sole defenders of the

Queen's English. Odd really because they break the *i* before *e* rule every time they write their names.

But it's during these alcohol-fueled debates that you can introduce this little challenge. Point out how British tourists seem to have problems with pronunciation. They are always talking about tomahtoes. Or nyuclear. Or aeroplanes. Most of them never quite get it right. In fact, there's one word that every Englishman pronounces wrong – no exceptions. Every single one of them and you bet that neither Einstein or Keith can guess what it is. And you can find it in every English dictionary, a copy of which, by sheer coincidence, you happen to have with you. You throw the pocket dictionary onto the table along with your challenge.

Usual fees apply. Education doesn't come cheap.

THE CATCH

When they've given up calling out difficult words from the dictionary in bad British accents, you flip through the pages to the *w* section and put your finger on the word "wrong."

"That," you say with confidence, and the best British accent you can manage, "is the one word that every Englishman pronounces 'wrong.'"

18 SPIN ON IT

THE HOOK

"Have you noticed how different coins have different sounds?" you say. You take out some change and start spinning it on the table as if proving something. So what? What you're actually doing is maneuvering Einstein into a betting position. He's been there all evening talking with Marilyn, and for the last half hour you and Mickey have been sitting with empty glasses and almost empty pockets. The last of your change is spinning like copper ballerinas on the table and adding it up you see that there's not even enough to buy a bottom-shelf rum and coke. So you make your challenge.

"I bet I can guess the date on any coin Marilyn pulls out of her purse – without even seeing it. All she has to do it spin it on the table while I'm not looking and I'll get pretty close. Even if I'm not exactly right, I'll guarantee that I'll be able to get closer than you, Einstein." That's some bet and it's not long before you, Einstein, and Mickey are facing away from Marilyn while she spins a coin on the table. Each of you has one guess at the date. Nearest to it is the winner.

THE CATCH

As you might have guessed, since you and Mickey are both broke, you've contrived this little game together. Basically it's an ambush. Let Einstein call the date first and then you and Mickey call the year before and after it. The odds are that you or he will be nearest to whatever date is on the coin. You've agreed to share the winnings.

There's a tiny possibility that you might lose, but only if Einstein's guess is exactly right. If that's the case, you only lose a five-spot, since what you forgot to mention to your pal Mickey was that he shares the risk too. Got to be worth taking a chance at those odds, though.

19 TRUST ME, I'M A DOCTOR

THE HOOK

This scam was used years ago by an eminent London OB/GYN. The doctor used it to enhance his reputation and therefore his earnings. He appeared to have the uncanny knack of being able to predict whether his pregnant patients were going to have a boy or a girl. He was never wrong. Always right. And it was this remarkable feat that brought him a lot of wealthy clients.

You can use it to get yourself a reputation as a real Nostradamus as well as free drinks all year round.

THE CATCH

When this scheme was devised there was no known way of accurately predicting the sex of an unborn child. But the doctor in question would hem and haw and mumble some pseudoscientific nonsense and then verbally predict the sex of the child and write it down in his surgery diary.

When the child was born, the client would come back to visit the doctor. Half the time they would congratulate him on his powers of prognostication, bring gifts, and spread the word of his seemingly uncanny knack. The other half of the time they would say, "Well, you said that I was going to have a boy, but I actually ended up having a girl. I guess you can't be right all the time and at least she was healthy."

At this the doctor would look amazed, saying, "No, no. I definitely said you'd have a girl, not a boy." And then he'd open up his diary, turn to the date of their consultation, and point out his prediction. This was because he always wrote down exactly the opposite of what he told them at the time, so the prediction was always correct — if he was right with his original verbal guess than he didn't bother showing them the diary on their post-natal visit!

And that's what you do. Whatever you tell someone, write down the opposite in your pocket diary at the time. You can actually use this devious system to place wagers on all kinds of events. Elections and championship boxing matches are particularly good bets; the only criteria is that there are only two possible outcomes and that it is sufficiently far ahead in time for your sucker to have conceivably forgotten which option you originally guessed.

80 HELD FOR QUESTIONING

THE HOOK

"Hey guys, that Marilyn is as clever as she is cute." This will be news to Keith and Einstein but you continue. "She could whip both of you in a quiz. In fact I'd bet money on it."

This is highly unlikely since Marilyn thinks that quiz is spelled with a *k*, followed closely by a *w*. But, her spelling skills aside, you continue to defend her intellect, much to their annoyance.

Five minutes later and the dynamic duo are locked in a battle of brainpower with Marilyn. To everyone's surprise, they lose! You, as usual, win.

THE CATCH

What we're talking about here is a rigged quiz. Questions are written on small slips of paper and then drawn out of an ice bucket. Since you pull the questions out, Marilyn gets the easy ones while Keith and Einstein end up with problems that Ben Stein would struggle with.

The trick is to know which question is which and you do this by folding them differently. The slips of paper that have difficult questions are folded in half, the easy ones into quarters.

You write all the questions in secret. Or better still, prepare them at home. Then put them into the bucket and pull them out one by one. The way the papers are folded make it simple for you to pick out difficult questions for the brainy bunch and easy questions for Marilyn.

Now it won't be long before Keith and Einstein start to whine. But that's why you have been extra cunning in compiling the questions. You see, the ones you wrote for Marilyn are easy for her to answer, but not for anyone else: her mother's maiden name, where she went to school, her first pet, etc. If they complain, just read one of them out, adding Marilyn's name and saying, "Okay then, where did Marilyn go to school?" They'll eventually shut up. And pay up.

FIVE

PARTY ANIMAL

"THERE ARE TWO WAYS TO
MAKE MONEY FROM YOUNG PEOPLE:
ENTERTAIN THEM OR CHEAT THEM."
— MARGARET WISEMANN

81 SITTING TARGET

THE HOOK

It's party time. All your buddies are here but it looks like a *Night of the Living Dead* reunion. A few party tricks – that's what this place needs. Something to catch the attention of the cute redhead sitting with the musclebound gym-monkey.

You could try this one on Dave, but he looks as though he's already comatose so it wouldn't be much of a challenge. Anyone who's sitting down will do, but if you don't want to expend too much effort then pick someone smaller than yourself. That buddy of Dave's, Ben. He'll do.

First thing is to get Ben to put his drink down. Then ask him to sit up, back straight, just like he was taught at school. Here's the challenge. You bet that he can't stand up from his chair in one movement without using his hands.

Let him try. It's easy enough. Bend legs, push up, keep the back straight, hands out of the way, don't move your feet. It's not particularly easy, but it's not impossible. "Okay, try it again, but this time I bet I can keep you in that chair using just one finger." You extend the forefinger of your right hand and flex it in a puny attempt at a display of strength. "One finger and you won't be able to get up. Ready?"

You flex your finger once more and press it lightly against Ben's forehead. You count to three and ask him to get up. Amazingly, he can't.

THE CATCH

As long as Ben adopts the posture you describe, he'll find it impossible to stand up if you press down on his forehead.

One point to watch is that the chair he's sitting on doesn't permit him to move his feet under his body. An armchair is ideal. People don't normally pay attention to the way they stand up. What they are doing is shifting the center of gravity by moving the body forward and the feet backwards. Normally the hands help push the body up from the chair too. Take all those aids away and you can render them incapable with the lightest touch.

82 PUSHING YOUR LUCK

THE HOOK

Wait a minute. The talk is getting all metaphysical now. Must be the booze. Or the boredom. But Marilyn's been jabbering about spirits and other worlds and Jim, who seems to be recovering from his tequila frenzy, is telling everyone how it's all true. Yes, multiple dimensions, how do we know what's real and what's not? All bull, but it makes a good introduction to this next bet.

"You're right. It's all a matter of perspective. A Tibetan monk showed me this once. It was amazing." You pull out a business card from your pocket. Not yours, of course. It's best not to leave any evidence. You fold it, tear a small hole in the middle of it, and then open it out again.

You peer through the hole at Marilyn as you say, "Yep, a Tibetan mystic showed me this. He could push a person right through a hole this size. Unbelievable huh?"

"Total nonsense," someone will say, quite rightly, and that's the person you make the bet with. "No, really, it can be done. I've seen it. I bet I can even do it myself. Ten bucks says I can push Marilyn right through this little hole, right here, right now, without tearing the card."

And with the money handed to Mickey for safekeeping, you proceed to do just that, push Marilyn through that tiny hole in the business card.

THE CATCH

Tibetan monk my ass. All the mumbo jumbo is just dressing to lead them off the track and antagonize some poor sap into calling you a liar. Serves him right when you make good on the bet by placing the business card against Marilyn's forehead and then prodding her by putting your index finger through the hole. You are *pushing her* through the hole and if you push hard enough she'll soon tell you to stop. No illusion there.

Smile as you do this one. You've just made an ass out of someone you hardly know. If you laugh it off, they should too. Doesn't matter how hard he laughs, though; he's still not getting his money back.

89 THE MONEY PIT

THE HOOK

That stunt with the hole and the business card is a winner. It's corny as hell but everyone's had a drink so they don't mind. As usual you pretend to feel a little bit guilty so you offer the sucker a chance to win his money back.

"I'll tell you what," you say, throwing three coins onto the floor. "Look at the hole and then look at the coins. All you've got to do is tell me which coins will fit through the hole and which ones won't. And I won't make the hole any bigger than it is now."

Sounds easy enough. There's a penny, a dime, and a quarter. That quarter will never fit through. It's obvious. It's also very strange because you've just bet him that if he can tell you which coins will fit through the hole, you'll give him back his ten-spot. But first, he has to put up another ten-spot to match the bet. I hope he's brought plenty of cash with him.

THE CATCH

The sucker will lose the bet because, strangely, all the coins will fit through the hole. It is an amazing thing to watch because you're about to put a large coin through a small hole.

With the penny and the dime you have no problem. The hole, if you've made it right, is slightly larger than the penny. They drop straight through. To get the quarter through you adopt a different strategy.

First you fold the card in half.

Then you drop the quarter inside so that part of it rests inside the folded hole but will not pass through. Next you push the corners of the folded card inwards. This results in the hole expanding in one direction. It has the same circumference but it is being squashed so that the diameter stretches. It will become large enough to allow the quarter to drop right through. Just make sure the card is thin and flexible. Instead of a business card, you can use a train or lottery ticket or anything similar.

The guy who paid out the ten-spot should consider it money well spent because he'll sure as hell be trying it at the office tomorrow.

84 CUT AND RUN

THE HOOK

Now's the time to lighten his wallet even further.

"I was just kidding. The fact is that I really can make a hole in a card and crawl right through it. Some say it's a mind-over-matter thing. But I say it's just dedication, healthy diet, and a pure heart."

That should bring the sneer of derision that it deserves. But you persist with your claim. First, though, you need a postcard and some scissors. Dispense a minion to find them while you keep your bankroller in plain sight and talk up the bet some more.

"Yep, I bet that I can cut a hole in this card and crawl right through it. None of that fake pushing stuff. I'll start on one side of the card and I'll crawl right through it to the other."

You're offering a real freak show tonight and no mistake. And with the postcard and scissors in hand, the sucker's going to need to put up the price of a ticket.

THE CATCH

In this bet you fulfill your promise to the letter. You really can cut a hole in a postcard (or any similar size piece of paper) big enough to climb right through.

To do it, though, you need to cut the hole in a very special way. First, make a horizontal slit as shown below.

Fold the card in half along the line of the slit and then start to cut straight lines across it from the top almost to the bottom. Between these you alternate with lines cut from the bottom almost to the top. Make the cuts as close together as possible. It's a fiddly job, but there's a tenner at stake, so take your time.

Now gently open out the card and you'll find that you now have a large loop. Handle it gently as it's very fragile and will break easily. But, if you're careful, you will be able to drop it over your head and slide it right down around your body.

85 PICKUP PUTDOWN

THE HOOK

That gorgeous redhead still hasn't noticed you. And the gorilla she's talking to has already arm wrestled everyone in the room, performed push-ups with one little finger, and now he's sitting at the table letting her feel his pecs. He's a babe magnet and it's beginning to annoy you because the nearest thing you've got to a six pack is the pile of empty cans next to you.

Never mind, there's one way you can share the limelight and make a few bucks on the side. You guessed it, it's time to move on to pastures new and pull a few more scams.

Tap the Hulk on the shoulder and ask how much he weighs. Don't be surprised if he knows exactly; that sort of person usually does. Tell him you thought he was lighter than that – that'll worry him. They always want to be heavier. Then look at the chair, look at him, and say:

"I bet I can lift you with one hand."

"What?"

"Lift you. And the chair. I bet I can reach down, grab that chair leg with one hand, and lift you right off the floor. For at least thirty seconds."

He will stare at you like the nut-job you're doing a good impression of. Especially if he remembers that you couldn't open the peanuts earlier on. But you look him straight in the eye and repeat your challenge. "Yes, I reckon I can do it. Lift you and the chair, straight up." Then wink at the redhead, and look back at him. Open your wallet, take out a ten-spot, and whack it on the table as you say, "If I'm wrong, you owe me a tenner. Is that fair?"

It's the equivalent of a slap in the face with a wet fish, and his ten-spot will soon be on the table right next to yours. In a moment, they'll both be cuddling up together in your wallet.

THE CATCH

Okay, get ready for this. If you want that tenner, you need to put on a performance that De Niro would be proud of, should he ever be seen dead at a party in Queens. With the money down, stand next to the Hulk's chair and eye it as if judging just how you are going to make the lift. Caution him:

"Hey, hands off the table, no cheating. This is hard enough as it is. If I'm wrong, you owe me a ten-spot, and that's ten bucks I'm not going to lose."

Look slightly mentally unstable at this point. Take off your jacket. Flex any muscles you can find. Snap a potato chip in two or burst a balloon as a warm-up. Grunt a bit and a crowd will start to gather. Explain the challenge to them. Don't begin the lift until you have plenty of people watching – they might come in useful later.

With your audience around you, repeat the challenge a final time to the Hulk: "Remember; if I'm wrong, you owe me a ten-spot." Now for the big sell. Kneel down by his chair. Put out your hand, grab the chair leg, and lift. Not too hard or you'll get a hernia. Just pretend to lift, because, let's face it, you haven't got a chance in hell. But it's all in the acting, as you step back and say, "Okay, last chance. You owe me a ten-spot if I'm wrong." Appeal to the crowd like J-Lo flashing her backside. They'll cheer you on, especially the redhead – women tend to go for feebleminded men facing impossible odds.

Now by this time anyone normal might have figured out what's going on. Even the redhead might be giving a little giggle. But a man that spends too much time in a mirror-lined gym isn't listening. Pretend to lift again. Not too hard. Then step back, wipe your brow in mock exhaustion, and say, "Okay, I admit it, I *am* wrong...you owe me a ten-spot!" Pick up the money, put on your jacket, and slowly walk away. It may take a moment before he realizes what happened. But the crowd will get it immediately. Which is good because they are the only thing that stops him from lifting you off the floor with one hand.

86 AGAINST THE WALL

THE HOOK

At last you've got some attention. Unfortunately it's mostly from the would-be Schwarzenneger whose money you've just filched. You suggest a rematch to even the score, reminding him of the old phrase "Find a penny, pick it up, and all day long you'll have good luck." In this case the penny will be replaced by his ten-spot, which will prove to be anything but lucky for him.

"You look like you do a lot of exercise. This should be a cinch for you. You can have your money back from the last bet if you can pick it up off the floor." Sounds too easy. Naturally there are a couple of conditions, the first being that he matches the money you are kindly putting up for this wager. The other rules concern the specific way he's got to do it.

"First, you stand upright." This could be a bit of stretch for the Missing Link. "And to make sure you are, stand over there, heels and shoulders touching the wall." Lead him over and make sure he assumes the position, pressing him back if you need to. Place the bill on the floor right in front of him.

"Second, you don't move your feet and you don't bend your knees. It's a straight pickup from the floor. Got that?" If he's done any gym work at all, he'll not think that's much of a challenge. The guy knows he can touch his toes without wincing. Picking up money off the floor shouldn't be a problem. Should it?

THE CATCH

This works well on any gym-monkey because it's much harder than it sounds. You place the bill just a few inches in front of him. Repeat the rules about standing straight against the wall, keeping his feet in position, and especially not bending at the knees. Then, on the count of three, ask him to try to pick up the ten-spot. If your instructions are followed properly, he will not be able to do it. Gravity will topple him over before he gets anywhere near the money.

It looks so strange that within minutes the rest of the room will be trying it. And you'll be sorry you didn't make the bet with all of them.

87 HAND OVER FIST

THE HOOK

If you're feeling brave, you might want to play the Hulk at one more game before sending him on his way a broken man. Ask him to clench his hands into fists, assuming he's not already doing that, and place one fist on top of the other. The thumbs are on top.

"Now hold them there. I'm going to try to separate those fists no matter how hard you try to keep them together. I get three tries. Then you get three tries with me. The wager is that I'll be able to manage it and you won't."

Since the Hulk is twice your size it would appear to be another bet in his favor. Surprisingly, you separate his fists on the first try. Oddly enough, he doesn't seem to be able to separate yours at all.

THE CATCH

Before you try this bet, make sure you haven't frustrated him enough so much that he uses this bet as an excuse for a punch in the nose. It's not worth it for a ten-spot.

But if he's up for some fun, you'll find that no matter how big he is, it's very easy to knock his fists apart. You just hit the back of the upper one firmly with your strongest hand. Slap it sideways and it will come off the top of the other fist. Don't punch though; otherwise he's liable to punch you back twice as hard.

The reason he can't knock your fists apart is that you cheat. As you put your right fist on top of your left, you secretly extend your left thumb and grasp it in your right hand. The thumb locks the fists together and a single blow won't be able to separate them.

FEET UP

THE HOOK

If the partygoers are laughing, you can get away with almost anything. Alcohol and laughter are an effective lubricant for the wallet. No one minds paying for a good time, and so when you offer to use your hypnotic powers to glue someone's foot to the floor, you'll find no lack of takers.

"It's true. It's a sort of magnetic influence. I just make a few mystical passes over your leg, and your foot will stick to the floor."

When someone dumb or drunk enough to accept the bet has put herself and her best foot forward, stand her with her side against the wall. "It's safer this way. Because sometimes the magnetic forces weaken the other foot and you might fall down." This is bull but you need to set up the conditions under which the bet will work. "If you feel yourself falling, you can hold onto the wall." Sure.

Jenny rushes forward to offer her appendages for the demo and you start making mysterious passes along her leg, commanding it to become "heavy, very heavy" as if trying to hypnotize her shapely limb. And no matter whether she's wide awake or blind drunk, when you finally snap your fingers and give the command, she won't be able to lift her foot from the floor. And all done without the aid of a nailgun!

THE CATCH

This is another stunt that uses the victim's center of gravity against her. The mystical mumbling is all nonsense but it's still important. To work the bet successfully you should use as much showmanship as you can manage. If people believe you are using hypnosis, the trick works even better.

Obviously hypnosis isn't actually necessary at all. It's the positioning of the sucker that's vital. She should be standing with her right side against the wall. The side of her right foot is against the baseboard. Her right shoulder touches the wall. This is supposedly to make sure she's upright and, as mentioned earlier, to stop her falling over. The real reason is to make her stand with all her weight on her right foot.

It's the left leg that you pretend to hypnotize, waving your hands up and down it like a demented Jim Carrey. Build dramatically to the actual moment, saying, "When I count to three, I'll snap my fingers and I want you to try to lift your left leg. But no matter how hard you try you won't be able to lift it without falling over. Here we go: one, two, three!"

Snap your fingers and shout, "Now! Your foot is stuck to the floor, your foot is stuck to the floor, your foot is stuck to the floor." The repetition helps unnerve her and when she tries to lift her left foot, she won't be able to without falling over. Like the gentleman that you are, you'll be there to grab her. And her boyfriend's cash.

STOLEN KISS

THE HOOK

Her man will be regretting backing his fiancée to take part in one of your dumb stunts. Time to put that animosity to good use. Get someone to find a sheet of newspaper. Lay it on the floor and make your next bet as leggy Jenny picks herself up off the floor and readjusts her skirt.

"I bet that I can stand Jenny and any man here on this sheet of paper and yet he won't be able to kiss her. Jenny on this side of the paper, him on the other. Both facing each other. And yet, after a few magnetic moves, he won't be able to plant a smacker on her lips."

Now most of the guys in the room have had a crush on Jenny since grade school, so even at a tenner you won't be short of volunteers lining up to take a crack. But both her lip gloss and your cash are safe.

THE CATCH

Once again, no magnetic powers are in effect. It's 100 percent scam. As soon as you have a challenger, lead him, Jenny, and the newspaper over to the nearest doorway. Place the paper on the floor in the middle and ask Jenny to stand on the far end of it. Close the door on her. The challenger stands on the newspaper too, but on the near end, this side of the door. With the door between them, you've just created one of the world's most effective contraceptives. You've also just won the bet. They're standing on the same piece of paper, face to face, and yet no kiss will come to pass. Her boyfriend should be grateful. Maybe even enough to forget the ten-spot you took off him.

TRIAL SEPARATION

THE HOOK

Jenny's being a good sport as usual and so you decide that there's room for another challenge with another kiss and another ten-spot at stake.

"No doors this time. Just my mystic powers of hypnosis. Jenny, I want you to raise your hands like this and place your fingertips together. Good. Here's the challenge. I'm going to make a few more magic moves and I bet that no man here will be able to pull Jenny's hands apart. Any takers?"

The Hulk would be a good bet for this but he's probably still smarting too much from his ritual humiliation. If people are slow in coming forward, up the stakes by saying, "And there's a smooch in it for any man that succeeds. From Jenny, obviously!"

Again it seems like an easy bet to win. Jenny is perfectly proportioned but definitely on the petite side. So when some lumbering doofus offers to take up the challenge, it looks like Jenny will end up swapping spit after all.

THE CATCH

When the sucker steps forward, position Jenny so that her hands are fingertip to fingertip. Her arms are bent and raised so that her elbows are almost shoulder height with her hands at the same level in between. Ask her to press her fingertips together as hard as she can, as you make some more of your phony mystic passes as if to imbue her with supernatural strength. If the guy is ugly enough, that should provide her with some motivation. If not, give her a wink and promise her half your winnings.

The guy is to grip Jenny's arms at the wrists. Tell him to take hold and try to pull her hands apart. He's not allowed to suddenly jerk them apart. He must use strength, not surprise, to separate her hands. That's the only condition.

No matter how hard he tries, even the biggest guy won't be able to budge her, and no one will be more surprised than Jenny. The more the guy tries to separate her limbs, the more determined she will be to keep them together.

⑨① GETTING THE NEEDLE

THE HOOK

Should anyone take your claims seriously – and never underestimate people's capacity to believe in utter crap – he might ask you about the way hypnosis is used to do all sorts of other marvelous things. Controlling pain for instance. It would be unethical for you to demonstrate pain control on a human subject, even if he has been anesthetized by a dozen bottles of beer. If, however, someone would care to find you a needle, you might be persuaded to give an alternative demonstration of your otherworldly powers.

You also need a few balloons; at a party they should be readily available. Grab a few and when the needle arrives make another bet.

"I can hypnotize this balloon so that it will feel no pain." If you've got a marker handy you might want to draw a face on the balloon. It's a bit of showmanship that will draw a bit more sympathy and appreciation from the hard of thinking. "This is Bob the Balloon," you say, bobbing the balloon up and down for emphasis. "And this is a needle, sworn enemy of balloons the world over."

Hand the needle to someone standing nearby and the balloon to someone else; preferably someone of a nervous disposition. Ask the person with the needle to stick it in the balloon. This will take some coaxing, especially of the person who's holding the balloon. When needle and balloon meet there will be the prescription bang. Bob is no more.

"A terrible tragedy, I think you'll agree. But I bet that, using hypnosis, I can stick the needle into a balloon and it won't go bang. Wanna see me do it? For a ten-spot?"

THE CATCH

Everyone is so used to the fact that if you stick a needle in a balloon it will burst that they don't think it could be any other way. That is, everyone apart from the smart-ass who remembers the old trick from their schooldays in which you secretly stick a piece of Scotch tape to the balloon beforehand and push the needle through that. But that would be cheating, you point out, and you would never stoop to such underhand methods – you're about to do it without any external aids or safety net.

The secret is where you stick the needle. At the top of most balloons,

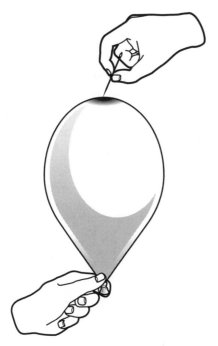

opposite the neck, you'll find that the rubber is considerably thicker and less taut. That's where you stick the needle. You've got to insert the needle carefully and slowly but you'll be amazed the first time you try it. The needle goes through the rubber and the balloon doesn't pop. It doesn't pop when you take the needle out either; it just deflates slowly as air pours out of the hole you just made.

Look around for the right type of balloon before you make the bet. You want one that's not inflated to its full capacity. And be sure to find someone really wimpy to hold the balloon the first time round. It all adds to the fun and, once again, the people who are laughing aren't thinking too much about how much money they're losing.

HARD CASH

THE HOOK

The next time you head out to get another beer, grab a handful of pencils from the junk drawer in the kitchen. Ask someone to hold one of them at each end and then ask someone else to lend you a ten-dollar bill. You should have wads of cash by now but you just tell them that they would think that you were cheating if you used your own money.

While you were learning your psychic skills and the secrets of hypnosis from Tibetan monks you were also fine tuning your martial arts skills. You became so adept at them that you can shatter wood with nothing more than a creased banknote.

You fold the ten-dollar bill in half lengthways and hand it around for scrutiny. "It's just a ten-spot. But the edge is sharp. So sharp that when I strike it against that pencil, it will slice through it like a knife through butter."

It's a dramatic claim and anyone looking at the bill and pencil will doubt it immediately. Doubt it enough, you hope, to make a wager.

THE CATCH

This is a joy. One of the best feats of skill around. There's no way that you can strike the pencil with the tenner and break it in two. But there is a way that you can fake the entire thing.

You hold the creased ten-spot between your finger and thumb. Make sure your sucker is holding both ends of the pencil as firmly as possible. After a couple of practice swings you slowly raise the bill in the air and then equally slowly bring it down towards the center of the pencil. Make it look as if you are gauging the exact spot at which to make your strike. Then raise the bill high again.

This time give out your best Bruce Lee yell and bring the bill down quickly against the middle of the pencil. What they don't see is that, as the bill descends, you quickly stick out your forefinger so that it's hidden behind the bill. It's the forefinger which actually breaks the pencil in two. The faster and harder you do it, the easier it is.

You won't believe how amazing this looks until you try it. As soon as your finger goes through the pencil, curl it back against your thumb and hand the bill out for further inspection. I've seen people totally shocked when they see this performed for the first time. It really is that impressive.

⑨③ HANDS DOWN

THE HOOK

Sit someone down and place their right hand palm-up on the table. Their forearm is horizontal and their upper arm vertical.

The challenge is for them to lift their hand from the table and then place it back palm downwards without rotating their wrist. It might not be entirely clear what you mean so let them try it first, and every time they rotate their hand at the wrist, point out that it's not allowed. "No, the challenge is to turn your hand palm down without rotating your wrist. You might think you could stand on your head and put your head on the table that way. But that's another thing you can't do. You've got to stay sitting down and maneuver your hand so that it ends up palm-down instead of palm-up."

This will drive them nuts. If they've never seen it before it seems utterly impossible. But it can be done.

THE CATCH

It helps to pretend that you're a robot for this one. Imagine that your right arm is mechanically hinged with no rotating joints. That's the way to defeat this strange challenge. It takes six moves to get your hand from palm up to palm down. Follow carefully:

 Raise your hand towards you so that it's at shoulder height, fingers almost touching your shoulder.

 Chop the hand down to the left, flat against your body in a vertical plane, with your elbow as the hinge. The finishing point of the move is with your forearm extended horizontally across your waist with your fingertips pointing left.

 Swing the forearm outwards horizontally until it extends straight out at ninety degrees to the waist.

♠ Once again bring the hand up towards the shoulder as in Step 1. The difference this time is that the palm of the hand is now facing left.

♠ Bring the hand down across the front of your body once again, as in the second step. This time the hand finishes palm down at waist level with the fingers pointing left.

♠ Keeping the upper arm still, swing the forearm out so that it points straight out horizontally from the body. This is just like Step 3 except you'll find that the hand is now palm down. Place it on the table. The challenge is complete. The hand has been moved from palm up to palm down without rotating the wrist.

94 THUMBS UP

THE HOOK

A game of Simon Says. You'll give anyone ten dollars if he can do exactly as you do. But if he can't, he can expect a sacrifice. Guess what that will be? There doesn't appear to be any particular difficulty to this challenge. You hold both arms out straight at shoulder height; he does the same. You turn your hands over so that the backs are facing each other. He does the same. So far so good.

Then you put one hand over the other and interlock the fingers, as in the prelude to the old "Here's a church, here's a steeple" routine.

Awkward but not difficult. What happens next, though, will leave the suckers gasping. Very slowly you rotate your hands at the wrist, turning them so that the thumbs are now pointing upwards.

Absolutely no one in the room will be able to follow this maneuver. Even putting their hand in their pocket to pay you will be far less difficult.

THE CATCH

If you followed the instructions you gave the suckers, you wouldn't be able to do this challenge either. Unusually for you, you cheated.

Give your instructions in the traditional Simon Says manner: "Simon says – hold your hands out. Simon says – clasp your hands together," etc. While the suckers are interlocking their fingers, you casually separate your hands again, using your right hand to gesture to someone at random, saying "not so high; a bit lower." Keep your left hand extended though. The seemingly helpful comment is just a bit of misdirection, because when you place your hands back together you don't place them back in the same position.

Instead, as it moves back, the right hand rotates a hundred and eighty degrees clockwise so that although the palm is facing to the right and the thumb pointing at the floor as before, the elbow is now pointing downward. Before you separated your hands, it was pointing upward. The right hand reaches under the extended left hand and the two hands clasp together once more, the fingers interlocking. This looks like the same position that everyone else is in. But it's not.

When you have both hands clasped you tell everyone to get ready for the final move – it's worth a ten-spot. "Simon says – bring your thumbs to the top." You do exactly as you say, rotating the hands slowly in an anti-clockwise direction bringing the thumbs to the top. Give them a waggle when they get there. And expect a big laugh from your audience, because they'll suddenly realize that they just can't follow you.

TONGUE TIED

THE HOOK

This is a great party game. Everyone throws some money into the pot and in return they're given a long piece of thread. They put one end of the thread in their mouths and let the other end dangle down to the floor. Hands have to be kept firmly clasped behind the back.

The object of the game is to eat the thread as fast as possible. They don't have to swallow it. In fact they'd be stupid to. No, all they have to do is chomp the thread up into their mouths. Whoever gets the thread into their mouth first wins the game. It's a test to see who's got the best tongue coordination. Who at a party could fail to be captivated by that?

And when the game gets underway you see those people who really are orally adept. Look at how quickly they can wind that thread up. Jenny in particular is putting in a fine performance, yet you remain calmly detached. In fact you've not even started on your thread yet, but you'll still win this game in the most unexpected manner imaginable.

THE CATCH

Anyone trying to wind the thread up with his or her tongue is doing it the hard way. You can bide your time while all the tongue twisters reel their lines in. People will wonder why you are simply standing there with a piece of thread hanging from your mouth and not making any attempt to play. Instead you cheer your punters on, giving them every encouragement.

But, when it looks like someone is about to win, you play your masterstroke. You purse your lips around the thread and suck in a deep breath. This will hoover up the thread so fast that it immediately disappears from view and ends up inside your mouth. It's a stunning thing to watch. And it takes but a second to make you the winner.

They'll be choked; just make sure you're not.

96 DRESSING DOWN

THE HOOK

They're a well-dressed bunch at this party. Nice to see that they seem to have made a bit of an effort, but it's all a little bit too reserved for your liking. Time to loosen things up a bit, and where better to start than with Jim, a man whose idea of a wild night is undoing his top button.

"That's a nice jacket, Jim. Very nice. Looks a bit tight on you though. And heavy. In fact I bet you can't take it off, alone and unaided, in less than thirty seconds."

Now Jim knows that he can get his jacket off in less than thirty seconds. It's his trousers he has trouble with. Especially after three bottles of beer. And although he had a close encounter with one of those big funny cigarettes the students gave him earlier, he's feeling much better now and feels that he can easily beat your challenge. Thirty seconds? He'll manage it in ten. Just got to shake it off the shoulders and let it fall clean off his arms. He's thinking it's you that must have had a few drinks too many. Ah, but perhaps there's a catch; maybe you're planning on grabbing hold of him to stop him getting the jacket off?

"Don't worry, no one's allowed to touch you or your jacket; they're not allowed to obstruct you – or help you, either." Fair enough. Game on.

THE CATCH

As soon as someone says "Go!" Jim will take off his jacket but he'll wonder what the hell is going on when you take yours off at the same time. The answer is in the wording of the bet you made. "I bet you that you can't take your jacket off, alone and unaided."

He's not doing it alone because you've taken your jacket off too. There really is one born every minute.

GET KNOTTED

THE HOOK

Now that Jim's taken his jacket off you can relieve him of his tie too. Hand it to someone and ask them to tie a knot in it. "Very good. But did you notice that you had to use both hands to do it and that you had to put one end of the tie through a loop to make the knot?"

Of course they did, and are thinking "So what?" So you attempt to stimulate their interest by being even more obvious about it. "It's completely impossible to tie a knot without letting go of the ends. Try it." And for the next five minutes let everyone have a go at making a knot in Jim's tie without letting go of either end. It just can't be done. Such a thing would defy the laws of physics. At least that's the conclusion they reach after trashing Jim's tie. The laws of physics, however, are just one of the many laws that you break with disdain on a regular basis. The rules are laid down, the cash hits the table, and in less time than it takes to say "what a trick," Jim's tie does indeed have a knot in the middle and everyone, while not exactly blown away by your technique, has to admit that at no time did you let go of the ends.

THE CATCH

It's perfectly true that if you take hold of a tie, or a piece of rope or string, by each end, it's impossible to make a knot without letting go of one of them. Except for one tiny loophole, and that's if you make the knot in your arms before you pick up the tie, then transfer it!

How? Easy. Lay the tie on the table in a straight line. Now fold your arms and bring your hands down to the table one at a time, taking hold of an end in each. Now, as you slowly unfold your arms, a knot will appear in the middle of the tie. It might not be the most impressive display, but we'll take their money first; their adulation can come later.

98 TIE MASSAGE

THE HOOK

After your suckers have seen you work *Get Knotted*, they might think they're a little wiser, albeit poorer, for the experience. They're astonished at your nerve, but then you offer to repeat the stunt, but with the following conditions: "This time I won't fold my arms. I'll hold the ends of the tie before I start. I'll make a proper knot. No play on words. And you can check everything to make sure it's absolutely fair and square."

You can let the suckers interrogate you for ages about this one and you're able to meet pretty much all their conditions. But the knot will stay in their imagination until they plonk down their money. After that, it will become frustratingly real.

THE CATCH

This is clever. You really will tie most of the knot while not letting go of the ends of the tie. It's only at the end that you employ a little swindle to make the impossible possible. Let's start with the moves.

Take the tie and hold it between your hands. Keep your left hand still and move your right hand over the left and back under so that a loop of the tie is draped over your left arm as shown on the next page.

You'll see that two gaps are formed at A and B. Your right hand now takes its end through gap A, around the middle of the tie and comes back out through gap B, without letting go.

Slowly move your hands apart and you're left with the tie looped around each wrist, crisscrossing between your hands. So far the suckers have seen you do some cool if strange looking maneuvers. At least it looks as if you're trying to tie an impossible knot. But it isn't quite there yet. You need the sucker's assistance to make the bet work.

"And just to be sure I don't do anything sneaky, I want you to grab hold of each end of the tie." Let him take one end with his left hand and the other with his right. Supposedly you are handing the tie to him so that it's completely under his control. What he doesn't know is that, in doing this, he's just helped make the knot.

Leave him with the tie and them ask him to stretch it out between his hands. He'll be amazed and dismayed when he finds that there really is a knot in the middle.

🄌 PHONEY

THE HOOK

The party's almost over and it's time to settle a few scores before you leave. Main thing you need is that redhead's phone number but how do you go about getting it? She's the cutest girl in the place, but no one has a clue who she is. Suddenly you have an idea. A little scam that'll serve two purposes.

You start by talking about the sensitivity of women and how they're generally more tuned into spiritual matters than men. And that if you take a little time, you can, because you've practiced, psychically home in on a woman's thoughts. Just like that Mel Gibson movie. There'll be doubters in the room so you offer a demonstration.

"It needs to be someone I don't know. How about you?" you say, pointing to the redhead. "I'm not going to ask you anything about yourself, but I'd like you to think of something that I couldn't possibly know. Your cell phone number will do; write it down here. Don't let anyone see it." You give her a pen and something to write on.

Then you ask her to sit on a chair, the information face down on the table in front of her. "What you've got to do is relax. Just concentrate on the number and I'll call upon the spirits to whisper it to me. Maybe we could have the lights down for this?"

Turning the lights down doesn't raise any spirits but your own. Nothing like a romantic atmosphere for what will soon become a very intimate drama between you and the object of your desires.

In five minutes time, the redhead will be convinced that the two of you have a psychic bond, you'll have her phone number, and the guy next to her who bet you that you wouldn't get it will owe you a ten-spot. How's that for a ménage à trois?

THE CATCH

Remember the set up. The paper with the girl's telephone number on it is on the table, writing side down. She's sitting with her hands resting on the arms of the chair.

You start with some psychic nonsense in an effort to convince her that you do indeed possess strange powers. Stand or kneel directly in front of her. Extend the forefingers of each hand and gently tap her on her hands. "Can you feel that?" Of course she can.

Move your hands along to her forearms and stroke her there. "And can you feel that?" She says yes again, quite rightly wondering what you're up to. Ask her to close her eyes, and then move to her upper arm and stroke her there. "And that?"

You continue the intimacy (or intimidation, depending on which way you look at it), both hands moving at the same time and tapping her gently on the shoulders with more questioning. Then you stroke the sides of her head. Finally you place each forefinger gently on her eyelids. At least that's what she thinks you've done as you've been touching her with both hands throughout. What you've actually done is asked her to close her eyes and extended the forefinger and the little finger of one hand and placed them on her eyelids, leaving your other hand free.

With the free hand you put your finger to your lips to silence the party crowd so that they don't give the game away. While the girl has her eyes closed you pick up the piece of paper from the table and read her phone number silently to yourself.

As soon as you've memorized it, turn it writing side down again and bring your left hand up in front of her face. Extend your left forefinger as you remove your right fingers from her eyelids and move both hands away from her face at the same time. Simultaneously fold in your little finger and ask her to open her eyes.

The first thing she sees is your hands moving slowly away from her face, both your forefingers extended. If you play it right, she'll still be assuming that you had one finger from each hand touching her eyelids. She has no idea that you could have seen the writing on the face-down paper. Ask her to hold your hand for a moment while you have another one of your funny turns, staring a lot and mumbling while you pretend to contact the other side to find out the number she's written down. Repeat the number you memorized aloud, all except for the last digit, saying, "We don't want everyone to know, do we?" The rest is up to you.

GET SHIRTY

THE CATCH

It's the end of the night and you've taken them for everything apart from the shirts on their backs. Now there's an idea.

Surely not even you though could get the shirt off someone's back while he's still wearing his jacket, could you? You'd better believe it.

Einstein doesn't believe it for a second. "There's no way you can get someone's shirt off without them taking off their jacket first!" And Keith is soon joining in, demanding proof.

Bob agrees, so does Jim and a few of the others and pretty soon you have a revolution on your hands with everyone putting down money to see you take the shirt off a man's back, like that isn't what you've been doing all night. Keith, egged on by Einstein, demands you put your money where your mouth is. And no tricks this time.

"Okay, I'll take you all on. One-to-one odds. And Einstein, it's your shirt I'm taking so brace yourself." With some reluctance Einstein sits down and lets you undo the collar and cuffs of his shirt – "Because when this comes off, you don't want your buttons flying everywhere."

"Step back boys. This is it." No one moves. Surely, you're not really going to pull his shirt off? Everyone's certain that you're going to pull some silly sleight of hand or talk your way out of it. What you're definitely not going to do is pull that shirt off...

My God! There's a collective gasp as you grasp the shirt by the collar and pull it clean away. Who's your daddy?

THE CATCH

You've been building up to this all evening and you haven't disappointed. And it's all thanks to Einstein because you and he are in cahoots. Yes Einstein, your former enemy, has suddenly become your accomplice. Well, he wasn't happy about catching Keith kissing Marilyn; she's been his girl since school. With revenge on his mind, it didn't take much to convince him to go to the john and prepare for his starring role.

The preparation is easy. Your stooge takes his shirt off and puts it back on by draping it over his shoulders like a cape. He fastens the buttons down the front and the cuff buttons around his wrists but leaves his arms out of the sleeves. He then puts his jacket back on top as normal. If he keeps the jacket buttoned, no one will be able to see that he isn't wearing the shirt properly.

The real art is in persuading someone to place a bet, and your stooge has a hand in that too, egging on the suckers. When you apparently turn the tables on him and choose him for the stunt, no one will suspect that you've set up the whole scenario.

Don't be surprised if you see your stooge pulling a few stings of his own next time you're down at the bar though; the buzz you get from pulling off a good scam can be addictive. But then, you've probably already realized that by now!

For more information about the author visit
WWW.PAULZENON.COM